HOW TO BE ON TV

Published by
Sunday Books
London
in association with
Peter Grose Ltd
Monmouth
First edition, 1995

Printed and bound in Great Britain for Sunday Books and Peter Grose Ltd by The Bath Press, Avon

HOW TO BE ON TV

By Chris Greenwood

Published by
Sunday Books
London

in association with
Peter Grose Ltd
Monmouth

Contents

New Telly Stars, Start Here 1
What Do You Want To Be? 7
Get To Know The Game 16
Star Target 27
Now You Try 38
Inside Job...Wheel In The Trojan Horse 50
All Change For The Starlight Express 62
Hit Them With Ideas 72
Play The Game 81
Make 'Em Laugh 91
In The Soap...And The
Confessions Of Miss X 105
Get Out And About 119
Now For The Good News 129
The Glamour Road...
And Other Routes 138
The Casting Couch 146
Have I Left It Too Late? Or
Am I Too Early? 155
Fame...A Fickle Butterfly 165

NEW TELLY STARS, START HERE

You want to be a telly star? I don't blame you. Look at the life style. Rarely cardboard city, is it? Home for the gogglebox royalty is always swish, judging by the pictures we see in the magazines when they are interviewed at home. Snooker tables, swimming pools, sumptuous sofas, gold His-and-Hers towel rails.

No wonder they can afford this kind of luxury, because look how they earn. When the big new contract is signed the salary is always in millions. And should the glittering wage earner hint that maybe the rival network is quite tempting, an extra wheelbarrow full of dosh is whisked around to the ivory tower so quick the tyres nearly catch fire.

Look how they love. Have you ever seen a TV star with an ugly bed partner? We're taking seriously beautiful people here. And amazing sex usually. "Kinky Kev had me in the boot of his Merc" confides the awesomely pretty Bimbo as she tells the press about her illicit fling with a randy soap star.

And there's another thing—look what they drive. Never a Robin Reliant or Ford Escort. TV stars get around on the best wheels. Back to that Here's-little-me-at-home-viewers feature we were talking about earlier. There'll be half-a-dozen nice little motors in the driveway, with a further batch locked away in the cavernous garage. And the jeep and the coupe will be freebies because the manufacturers just love to see the celeb cruising town in their product. Great PR.

I'm preaching to the converted. By this time you are champing at the bit and crying "Yes, yes....I know. That's why I want to be a TV star". Well, this is your fairy godfather speaking, and the good news is that you *can* make it big on the box. I'm not able to wave a wand over you and bring about instant magic. But I can do the next best thing and tell you how it is done. Read this book and you are on your way.

That's assuming of course that you are the right candidate for stardom. Here's a simple test. This morning when you looked lovingly at your reflection in the bathroom mirror while shaving or applying makeup, did you not already see the mirror as a TV screen? Did you not sigh to yourself and think what a waste that this beautiful and attractive person is going off to the office or factory and not to the studios to host some top-rating show?

This is a very basic requisite for TV stardom. You have to believe you are the right person for the job. You already have an ego which is a little bigger than the national average which will one day billow out into a massive stadium-sized dirigible.

So, once you realise you are star material, you have to go out and make it happen. No-one will do it for you. Maybe the heroes and heroines of soppy fiction get spotted by TV producers as they saunter down the street, but the chances of this happening in real life are about as remote as you getting offered a seat on the next rocket ship to the moon.

No point, either, in you asking advice from someone who has already done it. They ain't going to spill the beans. Why should they help train up the competition? It's a bit like giving a burglar the combination to your safe. But then you don't have to ask because I'm going to tell you all need to know. When I knew I was going to write this book I could have approached several very well-known TV stars and asked to talk them about how they got to the top. They would have laughed at me. But there was no need to go through all this because I already know all the answers to my own questions. I've worked with enough bigtime television personalities to know what they did to get to the stop, and what they are doing to keep themselves there.

I'll own up to actually approaching one star...Chris Evans, the bespectacled carrot-top who hosts Don't Forget Your Tooth brush. I don't know Chris and have never worked with him, but I am a great admirer. He is your classic self-made megastar. He didn't sit around waiting for fame to happen, he went out and grabbed it. He is what this book is all about. Chris is the new generation and I wanted to hear him spell it out for me. He turned me down...politely. I'm not surprised. In fact I was expecting it. It doesn't matter. It doesn't affect the thrust of this book one bit because, Chris mate, I *know* how you did it. I'm going to blow the whistle, spill a few beans. Like a friendly Frankenstein I stand here, test-tube in hand, ready to create a whole new generation of TV stars. You and your fellow glitterati will only be secure in your walled city for so long.

This book is described as an insider's guide and that's exactly what it is. I'm inside the starry castle and I'm going to drop the drawbridge for you. If you tried the usual route into television you'd probably drown in the moat, sinking under a dead weight of application forms and rejection letters.

If a job is glamorous there'll always be some ordinary little squirt who will try and deter you.

It's happened to me all my life and I've never let them put me off. As a lad I wanted to be a newspaper reporter. I asked the careers officer in my local North London town to give me advice, and he said: "Oh, everybody wants to be a journalist. You stand no chance. Go off and be a clerk". Instinctively I ignored the negative pratt. I wrote to every local newspaper in Greater London. All the editors said no, sorry. So I started sending in my own reports, following fire engines and police cars and in the end the editor of my own town weekly couldn't stand the harassment any more and he gave me a job as a cub reporter.

Then I set my sights on television. This was even tougher. The BBC didn't even bother to reply to my letters. Probably because I didn't have a degree. Or because my uncle wasn't an archbishop. Then someone gave me some great advice....the sort of good guidance you're going to find in abundance in this book.

I cracked it. And so will you. Get ready for the snazzy pad and the "Roller", Stardom's on its way. And just do me a little favour. When you are up there on the stage getting your BAFTA award and you are giving your thankyou's, wave your copy of this book in the air and shout “I learned it all here”.

I’m going to be so proud of you.

WHAT DO YOU WANT TO BE?

So, you've made the big decision. You are going to be a TV star. You've got one foot on the yellow brick road. In your mind's eye you've already had your first good review in the papers and hit the night spots with a very glam bit of meat on your arm.

Right, now here comes another little test. What are you described as in the press write-up? Soapie star Kev Kutebutt? Game show hostess Georgina Greatgussett? Rule one, make up your mind what type of telly star you want to be. If there is one important continuing theme running through this book, it is be clear about where you are heading and what you want to achieve, draw up your battle plan then stick to it like Araldite with Attitude.

Television is like a giant sweet shop. You walk in and everything looks tempting. If you don't really know what you want you'll grab for the first glittery jar that catches your eye and the contents could be quite wrong for you. In fact they might even poison you to death. I've lost count of the number of people who come up to me and say: "Oh, I'd love to be on telly" to which I reply: "Yes, like what?" and they sigh: "Well, you know..anything really."

These are the people who are destined to get nowhere. When thinking about television they have a general idea about a world that is very glitzy and glamorous and they want to be a part of it. More often than not, their concept of the industry is based on a daydream, which in turn will have been based on fiction they have seen on TV or film.

If they are young and physically attractive enough they might make it to a producer's bed for the night, only be put out the following morning with the milk bottles. There's a whole chapter of this book devoted to the sensitive and sensual subject of the casting couch.

When you start paying attention to your telly, which you now have to do in earnest, you will be surprised just how many people get their faces on your screen. For a start you've got the heavyweight megastars who host the popular family entertainments shows—Michael Barrymore, Cilla Black,

Noel Edmonds, Des O'Connor, Jeremy Beadle, Mike Aspel and co.

If you're a real smart-arse you'll have their jobs in your sights already, and good on you. Then there are the soaps—Coronation Street, EastEnders, Neighbours, Home and Away, Brookside and so forth. They have large casts whose faces and characters become very familiar to the public. The acting trade in general grabs a huge slice of screen time when, in addition to the soaps you consider straight drama (The Bill, Casualty) and comedy (Only Fools and Horses, One Foot In The Grave).

Next the game shows like Blind Date and Generation Game which not only have the big starry hosts but loads of contestants. Keep reading and further down the track you'll hit a whole fascinating chapter on the subject of how to get on telly as a game show contestant. Not only that, but how to use your exposure as a contestant to spring off into a more permanent TV job.

News and current affairs have their big guns—news readers like Trevor McDonald, Michael Buerk and Peter Sissons and star reporters such as Martin Bell, Kate Adie and Mike Nicholson. Documentaries have their star presenters too with Jonathan Dimbleby and co.

You also have a whole range of shows which we

in the business call 'info-entertainment'. In other words, lighten up a little as you learn. This takes in the regular morning shows like Big Breakfast, Ann and Nick and GMTV, and regional magazine programmes in the early evenings. Info-entertainment also covers motoring, consumer reports, cooking and showbiz.

Then there are the solo comedians, who either have their own shows, or who keep cropping up as guest stars on other people's shows, or both. These are the Paul Mertons, Victoria Woods, Rowan Atkinsons, Ruby Waxes, Brian Conleys and Julian Clarys. Don't forget the sporting set...Des Lynam and the like. And the weather prophets—Michael Fish and the meteorological mafia.

If you spend a week glued to your set you'll pick a few more categories too. And you will realise what a wide choice there is. So, how do you choose? Well, you have to ask yourself a few frank questions. The first one is easy...whose job would you like? This is called "star targeting" and you'll be hearing more about this very soon. My bet is that if you have gone as far as to buy this book, there is someone on telly you'd love to be. Is it Phillip Schofield? Ulrika Jonsson? Mel Smith? Magnus Magnusson? Matthew Kelly?

Next question is, can you do it better than them?

Don't be frightened or ashamed if you hear yourself crying out "Of course" because you're only showing the right type of ego that will eventually propel you to the top. In fact if you have a seriously big head you might look through the week's programme schedule and see *no-one* as good as you. Or as good as you could be if you had your own show.

Right, so you think you've found the type of show you want to host. Now ask yourself, can you hack the working conditions? Remember the old lags make it look very easy. When Bruce Forsyth says "I'm in charge" he is. Bruce is a brilliant controller of people—one of the best you'll see anywhere in the world. Handling ordinary folk who have usually never been on television before he cajoles, bullies and guides them into prime time performers. He has an instinctive knack of knowing how to handle each individual. If you are another Bruce Forsyth someone at sometime will have said how good you are with people.

You might have been MC at a friend's wedding, or captained the winning team at charades during the office Christmas party. You will have displayed a talent for encouraging shy people to show off a little, and held back overbearing oafs who want to hog the show. In a not-too-displeasing way you will have dominated the proceedings with your personality. You might have even heard the magic words "you should do this professionally".

Forsyth is essentially a comedian, as indeed are the hosts of many popular family shows. Do you tend to make people laugh a lot? Does it happen easily? Can you do it without resorting to a joke, with a mannerism or silly face or observation that is one hundred per cent your own? If you are nodding away madly to all this, then you could well be another Forsyth or Monkhouse in the making.

What about acting? Here's a test. Have you made the first move yet? Have you ever performed anywhere in public? Have you starred in amateur dramatics? If you haven't, are you prepared to give it a try? If you are serious about taking up acting as a profession, are you prepared to quit your regular day job and live dangerously? Remember that for every player currently strutting their stuff in Coronation Street or EastEnders, there are another ninety-nine out of work. Not that this is intended to put you off, just a warning that challenges lie ahead.

If you fancy Trevor McDonald's desk, do you actually follow the news closely? How many newspapers do you read each day? How many bulletins do you catch on TV or radio? When a fire engine rushes by, do you ever feel tempted to follow it? When you watch an evasive politician being interviewed do you shout your own questions at the screen? You do? That's a very good sign.

Maybe it's the consumer watchdog for you. Fancy yourself as another Roger Cook? Well, how's your bottle? If a gang of burly builders have ripped off a relative or neighbour, do you have the nerve to go down to their yard, kick in the door of the tea hut and demand justice? If your steak is like shoeleather and the lager is warm, do you get the waiter back and kick up merry hell? Every time you buy a new car or appliance do you put the salesperson through the hoop, making absolutely sure you are getting the very best deal; or, more to the point, not getting conned?

What about the travel that goes with the roving reporter's job? Would you really relish jumping around the world from one trouble spot to another with barely enough time at home to rinse your underpants through? What about initiative? Could you wangle a camera team and yourself into a particularly tricky country when they discover at the airport that you don't have the right paperwork? How brave are you? Those were real bullets whistling overhead when you saw the reporter standing there sending a despatch from Bosnia or the Gulf War.

Now for sport. How wide is your range of knowledge and interest? You might be a whiz at footie and the gee-gees but what about tennis and athletics? Or motor racing, boxing and skiing? The top commentators have to be clued up on all popular sports. They can't afford the shrug their shoulders and say: "Yuk, I just can't stand hockey". If the boss heard that they'd be down the job centre double quick on the roller skates.

And cooking. How would you be in Keith Floyd territory? You might like cooking, but have you ever thought of doing your souffles and sausage rolls in front of an audience? In fact have you ever tried cooking and talking at the same time? Are you a good cook only in terms of recipes you have learned from other peoples' books, or do you get original ideas? You'll be hearing me bash away quite a lot about the importance of bright ideas and original thought as we progress towards getting you on screen.

I'll also be covering the crucial question of whether or not your looks, your personality and even your name are suitable for the on-camera job you fancy. If you want to front Top of the Pops or a similar type of show you have to look in the mirror and ask yourself; do I look the part? Imagine an off-camera announcer shouting out your name to introduce you. Does it have the right ring? And also, as with sport, do you have a really wide knowledge and appreciation of all sorts of popular music?

So the message is simply this: think carefully about

what each on-camera job entails. Are you really cut out for it? And be warned—don't ask anyone else, because they will probably have the wrong idea. Or they might laugh out loud and put you off altogether. Eventually you are going to have to face a lot of cynicism when news gets out that you intend to get on telly. You're not quite ready for all that flak just yet. You need to build a bit more inner strength.

It might well be that once you crack the job you are aiming for you might well switch to something else. Terry Wogan went into the business as a radio DJ, switched to telly as a game show host with Blankety Blank and finished up with his own chat show. Noel Edmonds had a similar switch, starting on Radio One and ending with his own highly successful House Party. This doesn't alter the fact that you should still have your eye on one particular goal for beginners.

The big battle is going to be getting that face of yours on the box. Once you are there and making a success of it, who knows what other offers you might get. If you shine in your new Coronation Street role you might well catch the eye of a Hollywood producer. Let's get you into the Rovers Return first.

GET TO KNOW THE GAME

Now you know what you want to be you have to start learning about the television business, how it works, who does what, with which and to whom. Don't be intimidated by the task. There are weighty volumes already written on the subject which would be enough to put anybody off. These books make television seem like some far-off planet that only the most gifted and academically brilliant flyers can reach. There'll probably be mention of special courses you don't stand a monkey's of getting on, and a whole load of people to write to who will either ignore your letter altogether or send you a form as thick as a telephone directory which makes no sense.

I say probably because I've never read any of these books. I've never filled in a form to get a job in my life. I got into television my way, which is a damn sight less complicated than all that formal crap, and a lot more exciting. This is the route I'll be showing you. Which is why at this stage I don't want you to be put off.

Avoid discussing your plan to crack TV with anyone who is negative or mocking. You don't need people like this. I'm sure that when Sir Edmund Hilary first started putting out the idea that he was going to scale Everest there was some spineless twot who laughed "Come on, Ed. Get real."

The people you do need to start chatting up are those who work in television, or who have genuine knowledge of the game. This is an important part of the learning process. I'm writing now on a computer which I learned to use by asking friends and relatives who were already clued up. I also watched them in action. If I'd attempted to plough through the thick instruction bible that came with the machine you would have finally got to read this by the middle of the next decade.

With any jobs that are tricky, dangerous and a bit out of the ordinary you are going to do your most useful training in the company of those who are operating in the field. More often than not they are not even aware that they are teaching you. It's a question of getting in there near the action, and keeping your eyes and ears open. A couple of chapters down the track I'll be giving the lowdown on how to actually infiltrate a TV team, but in this early stage what you have to do is get a broad view of the battlefield.

So, your next move is to find someone who works in television, then get on side with them. If you say 'but I don't know anyone in the business' then you have got to start getting the old finger out and be a bit clever. If none of your friends or kin are in telly, then one of them could well know someone who is. Or know someone who knows someone who is. Bear in mind that when you are seeking this person there are literally hundreds of jobs in television. Don't just concentrate on the glamorous types you tend to read about most—the performers, directors, producers, cameramen, stuntmen and make-up artists. There are scene shifters, props buyers, video tape editors, caterers, electricians, lighting staff. Also a whole team of clerical workers who back up the industry. Their jobs might seem dull weighed up against Noel Edmonds', but they still know more about TV than you do.

Once you have located your victim, move in gently. If you start barraging them with leading questions they'll think you might be from the Inland Revenue...or worse, that you are after their job. If you can come up with a believable excuse to justify your interrogation it will make life a whole lot easier. Why not say you are on a creative writing course, and you have decided to do a project on television. To provide yourself with a front, enquire locally about evening classes and see if there is a writing course. If one exists and there is a vacancy, take it. The experience won't do you any harm. In fact it might actually help later in the game.

So, once it is known you are away at nights learning to be a writer, you have your excuse to get cracking on the real job in hand, even if during your actual classes they are boring you cross-eyed about Shakespeare or how to pen lovely prose about daisies in a spring field. Who's to know? If there is no evening class then scan the newspapers and find one of those postal courses. Send off for the bumpf. You don't necessarily have to sign up. It'll give you a convincing envelope and paperwork to leave lying around. If all this fails just say you are helping some youngster with a school project.

Right, so you've asked around, done a bit of ferreting, and struck gold. Your dart partner's auntie's plumber drinks with a bloke who shifts the scenery on the Barrymore show. Great. Eureka. Get over to his boozer quickly and start pouring beer down his throat. Then get him talking about his job. He probably likes to anyway. Most TV people do nothing else. If you have got some sort of semi-official reason, like the project you are on, then he'll like it even more. It's a bit like being interviewed for a newspaper.

Now, a bit of advice about the questioning. You want to get from this guy all he knows about how the Barrymore show functions. First and foremost, ask him in detail about what he does. OK, so he moves the scenery about but who tells him where to put it? Who builds it? What about the bits with flashing electric lights? Can they be dangerous to handle? Has anything fallen on his head? Has anything fallen on Barrymore's head? Where is it kept when it is not needed? And so on.

Then ask him what other people on the production team do, or seem to do. Gradually you will begin to get the picture of how television works, which will be crucial knowledge when you set out to infiltrate the business. For God's sake don't hint about this in your session with the scene hand, because he'll be convinced it is his job you are after.

So, you'll hear about the cameramen, and how they bump into each other when moving swiftly to change positions. About the director, up there in the control room, shouting obscene threats down everyone's earphones. About the make-up girl who swoops in and out of the action, dabbing sweat off Barrymore's face while making sure she keeps out of the camera's range. About the researcher, who is responsible for looking after one of Michael's chat guests, and might need a bit of special furniture to be moved on to the set before the sequence begins.

Next move is to get an invite to the show, to be in the actual audience when Barrymore is recorded. If you have become really chummy with the scene hand, then he will be able to arrange this for you through his connections at work. Tickets for top shows like Barrymore are always in demand and there is often a long waiting list. If he can't or won't, note which company makes the programme from the credits which appear on the screen when it is over. Then ring them up, ask to be put through to the audience ticket unit and do a heavy sell about how important this project is, how you have an exam coming up very soon, and must, just must get in to see Barrymore as soon as possible.

I'll help you out this time. Barrymore is made at London Weekend Television and the telephone number is 0171-620 1620. But I don't intend to get bogged down in long lists of telephone numbers, names of television companies and people to contact. Everything changes so quickly in telly. My list would be out of date as soon as it was published. In fact as I write this it isn't even certain that Michael Barrymore is coming back for another series at LWT. The company itself might be out of business, or calling itself something else by Christmas. So, you're going to have to keep yourself in touch and spend a bit of time on the old blower.

For argument's sake let's paint the grim picture

and say that you've rung LWT and found that Barrymore is no longer being produced, or that if it is, there are no more tickets for that season. Right, then hang in there with the ticket unit and ask what else is going on. What about Cilla? A lorra lorra fun there. But again, she's a popular lady and the tickets tend to go quickly. So, as the last resort, ask the ticket unit for anything they may have. You just need to get into that studio and start breathing the air.

So, all this hustling has worked, and you are finally queuing up at The London Studios on South Bank waiting to be shown in for a recording. Don't just stand there, get hold of one of the ushers and give a good excuse about why you must sit at the very front...you are deaf and have tunnel vision, you have a phobia about sitting behind other people, you need to keep flexing your gammy knee.

One of the reasons you need to be sitting at the front is because you are going to be much nearer the people who are working on the show. You'll be within a spit of the floor manager, camera and audio operators and all sorts of other interesting people. Let's say that the drinks with the Barrymore scene hand never took place, and this is your first encounter with TV folk. If you are subtle and time things right you'll be able to get into conversation with one of the technicians or production workers.

When I say time things right you are obviously not going to tap a cameraman on the shoulder just as he is focussing in on a dodgy shot like Barrymore whirling around on a unicycle. You choose your moment. During the recording of TV shows, there are lots of stops and starts. Things go wrong and have to be redone, tape needs changing, extra scenery needs to be brought in. You won't have to be a detective to know. Everyone will relax, and the warm-up man will come out and assault you with some terrible old gags.

Should you be smart enough to score a seat at the front of the audience ramp you will be close enough to a camera operator to call out, or even tap him or her on the shoulder. Start your conversation with something polite but technical to get them hooked. "Excuse me asking, but how do you make the camera go up and down so quickly?" You'll get some sort of reply. If you sense a chatty type pitch in deeper with questions about how they got started, what's going on in their earphones and so forth.

Just a little reassurance in case you think I've left the rails. No, you are not out to become a career cameraperson, you are learning about the trade and the people who make it tick. One day you will be the star the camera is pointed at. But knowing what people do behind the scenes will be a huge bonus when you are finally a performer. You will also be wise to respect them. Upset a make-up artist and she can make you look like death's doormat on screen. Likewise with the camera crew. Get them offside and you'll be shot so badly the producer will wonder why you were ever hired. And you might find yourself unhired.

So, you are chatting away to the cameraman or maybe the sound crew. Usually there is a boom microphone in use, strung on the end of a large retractable pole and dangled over the heads of the artists. The trolley from which the boom operates is normally parked near the audience. Whoopee. Another group of technicians to chat up. With a bit of charm you might even find out where they drink. Or play tennis. Or go formation dancing. Hang in there.

All is not lost if you didn't get the seat up front. Camera, sound and lighting crew move up and down the aisles during recording, and will often be standing there when things stop for a while. Grab the opportunity for a bit of a jaw. Don't be shy. You're going to be a star, remember, and that requires courage. If there is no-one in your aisle make an excuse to go and have a pee during the stoppage. On your way back, if recording hasn't resumed, hover on the edge of the floor before going back to your seat, and try and strike up conversation with anyone who looks like they are doing something interesting.

If you don't take too long about it, you should be OK. The worst that can happen is that a studio usher or a floor manager will tell you to go back to your seat. You'll only get slung out if you touch any equipment, or get stroppy. What you are exercising now is the gentle art of infiltration. You'll be quite an expert by the time you have read this book.

What you will also be experiencing is the excitement of being in a television studio, particularly if this is your first time. Unless you are a complete log it can't fail to move you. I have been in the business for nearly thirty years and I still get a huge buzz from being in a studio—particularly when the show is going out live. The atmosphere is so thickly charged you could bottle it.

With a little persistence, you'll get into a television studio somewhere, sometime while a programme is being done. Let's assume you can't, or there is a bit of a wait. There are other ways to get into a studio. Most big complexes have organised tours. You'll be herded around like sheep, and more often than not you won't be allowed in a studio while recording or transmission. Even so, don't sniff at it. At least you'll get an idea of how things work. And you'll get to talk to a few clued up technicians. Again, if they are really friendly, arrange for a beer or a coffee. Or if they are cute, a date.

In fact if you want to be really thorough do both—

the studio session and the guided tour. While you are on the plot you might even be lucky enough to bump into a star in the foyer, or in a corridor. Note the special vibes they put out, the sort of glitzy glow that exudes even though they might be in ordinary clothes and out of make-up. Look how people react to them.

If you don't want to be like that, turn back now, because that's the way you're heading.

STAR TARGET

Chris Evans is a classic example of a self-made telly star. He worked out for himself a lot of the moves I'm putting you wise to now. Chris gained a toe-hold in the business through clever infiltration, a tactic I'll be explaining later. He then targetted a particular star, which is what this chapter is all about.

Chris looked at oddball kids' host Timmy Mallet and thought to himself: "I could be like him—only better". So he set out to do just that. He targetted Mallet, with a view to learning all about him, then overtook him.

In motor racing they call this slipstreaming. You tuck in behind your rival, real close, taking advantage of the fact that his car or bike is having to force through the wind barrier. Then when the timing is right you pull out and whiz past.

Talk about getting in close. Chris pulled a masterstroke and actually finished up sorting Mallet's fanmail. He just rang up Piccadilly Radio in Manchester and offered himself for the job. Next thing, there he is breathing the very same air as the great man himself. Doing something menial for stars is a smart way to hang around in the right atmosphere until your own moment comes. Bette Midler was a cloakroom chick in a starry night club, Robert Wagner caddied for the top stars on the Hollywood golf links, and of course there was the carpenter Harrison Ford, who sorted out many a celebrity home in Beverly Hills.

Back to Chris Evans, and the case history of how he malleted Mallet. Evans was already a larger than life character before he got into fulltime showbiz. He was a very popular but eccentric newsagent in his home town of Warrington, and had run his own kissogram service and private detective agency. He looked at Mallet and saw blatant wackiness...clothes and hats of hideous colour and pattern, bizarre spectacles, squeaky voice, weird puppet companions. Above all there was an energy, an unusualness about Mallet which stopped you in your tracks and made you watch him even if you couldn't stand the fellow.

If you watch Chris work now on telly you have an energy fireball with vivid, carrot-coloured hair, mega-nerd specs and an unstoppable line in patter.

Love him or loathe him you can't ignore him. Even if you are striding across the room to find the remote and switch channels, you still have to stop and gawp a while. Television success is all about impact on the eyeball.

Over the years, since he quit Mallet's mailbag and progressed to his own radio and TV shows, Evans has taken his former master's identity and formed himself into a more sophisticated mutation. I don't think Mallet could, or would turn round and complain: "Hey, he's nicked my act." Evans *inspired* by Mallet would be a better way of putting it. Like McCartney in his early Beatles days inspired by Little Richard. Or Michael Barrymore by John Cleese.

So, who have you got your eye on? There must be somebody. Who's your favourite fireman in London's Burning? Got a nurse whose style you dig in Casualty? And Robbie Coltrane, what a Cracker he is. What about comedy?

There is an abundance of funny folk on TV, what with French and Saunders, Paul Merton, Lenny Henry, Ben Elton, Rowan Atkinson, Ruby Wax, Freddie Starr and a few score more.

Let's say for instance that you settle for Rowan Atkinson. What you see on your screens now is a comic in a classic tradition. He would have been equally at home 70 years ago when silent movies were all the rage. Rowan gets the laughs without uttering a word, which is the joy of Mr Bean. Each limb seems to have a mind of its own, the face contorts as if made of rubber. The things about him seem funny too. I laugh as soon as I see that silly little mini car.

You've got to look hard at Atkinson now and figure how how he does it. You're targetting him. I can help you with a little early research. Years ago I worked in the same room as Rowan. Some planning genius at the Beeb decided that the Parkinson chat show team would make suitable cellmates with the young loonies from Not The Nine O'Clock News. And so it was, with a series of screens dividing us. In those days you would never have picked Rowan as a star. A brilliant scholar, he was only recently down from university. And that's what he looked like, a student. Stick thin, with a shock of dark hair and wire-rimmed glasses, he came across as painfully shy. And very nervous.

What Rowan did have was an extraordinary way of walking and grimacing, particularly when he was agitated. We saw examples from time to time. In those days he was a heavy vehicle enthusiast. One day he had arrived in a juggernaut and had parked it on yellow lines outside the BBC television centre. Warning was telephoned through that the wardens were on their way. Rowan flew out of the office like a preying mantis on speed. I've never seen limbs move like it. We all fell about.

There was an even funnier demonstration a few weeks later. We all lived quite happily in the big room...until the fatal night Not the Nine O'Clock News decided to take the piss out of old Parky. There was a brutal parody of Mike's apparent passionate love of cricketer Geoffrey Boycott, to the point where the sexual act nearly happens during the course of the interview.

Next day we all had to be in the same room together. And the layout was most unfortunate for the NTNON team. A single door led into the room, and close to this door was the huge desk where Parky sat, overseeing his team like a headmaster. So the comedy crowd had to pass right by his shoulder to get to their side of the screens.

We all sat there in anticipation. No-one had dared mention the previous night's send-up. Then the NTNON people started arriving, late in the morning as usual. Mike busied himself with his research, head buried in hand. Passage past his desk was swift, except Mel Smith, who had the nerve to swagger in at his normal pace. Finally Rowan's frightened face appeared at the door. He looked at Mike, at us, then withdrew into the corridor. Then we witnessed the most amazing funny walk I've ever seen. It left John Cleese for dead. This was Rowan entering a room while trying to leave it at the same time. He sort of flattened himself against a wall and slid past the desk, his head kind of retracted into his body and arms and legs moving in all sorts of directions. He needn't have bothered, because our giggles and his contortions alerted Parky to what was going on. He stood up, smiled, and walked next door to congratulate them on a great show.

So, if you fancy yourself as a bit of Rowan Atkinson, there's probably something naturally funny about you already. Your loping stride, your gangly arms, your elongated head or your counter-rotating eyeballs. You have to exaggerate what's already funny. Rowan is a clever comic. He knows which of his body parts to use to best advantage. That marvellous face, for instance. The mouth is a star in its own right, and the eyes are like two mad planets, both hellbent on heading off to another universe. His nose is certainly big in proportion to the rest of his features, but when going for laughs he makes it seem almost as large as the rest of his body.

Right, so start watching Rowan in earnest. It is amazing what you'll spot once you have turned your viewing into a research project. As far as tools of the trade are concerned, I'm assuming you have a telly and a video. These are basic requirements for the course. Later you'll need access to a camcorder, too, but they are hirable. And now you have before you a pile of Mr Bean and Black Adder tapes, plus maybe an old Not The Nine O'Clock News, which you've borrowed from a friend's private archives. Play 'em all through. Then again. And Again. Watch Rowan like you've never watched before. When you hit a scene which really makes you laugh, find out what it was he did which tickled your funnybone.

With Mr Bean there's normally a particularly awkward situation which causes him to move in very strange ways. For instance, the time when he goes shopping, and at the pay desk his credit card finishes up in someone else's wallet. Mr Bean tries to gently fish the wallet out of the other customer's hip pocket...at which point the chap heads off. Mr Bean heads off too. He has no choice, because his hand is jammed in the hip pocket with the wallet. Which provides a lovely excuse to do a very funny walk. Rowan moving along but not wanting to be there, just like that day in the Parkinson office.

There are scores of classic Bean sequences. The beach scene, for instance, when he is changing from his street clothes into his bathers without any shelter and very aware of his own modesty. And the night when he is the lineup to meet The Queen Mother at a gala premier and his shirt front gets jammed in his flies in a very rude-looking way.

Rowan is wonderful in close-up, too. The face is a theatre show in itself. He is at his best in Black Adder when scowling, getting outraged with Baldrick or grinning creepily to try and get onside with the Queen. Note too that his characters aren't particularly nice people. Black Adder certainly isn't. And Mr Bean is the type of fellow who tries to leave a car park without paying. He is a soloist by nature and not a great lover of mankind.

Quite soon you are going to be doing a bit of the old Mr Bean yourself. I'll be telling you how next chapter. But as part of your get-to-know Atkinson campaign you need to do a bit of reading about him. If you are really nice and oily on the phone, you might persuade your favourite TV magazine to send you photocopies of some articles about him. If you say it is for a course or project your chances will be better.

When you read up about Rowan get a clear picture of every aspect of his life. What he was like as a kid. Did he show early signs of being a clown? When did he first start performing in public? What contacts did he make? Why did he decide to make certain moves in his career? Who were his influences? Did he have a star target when he was getting under way?

Be clear in your mind that you are not going to actually copy Rowan Atkinson and become a clone, just like Chris Evans didn't become Timmy Mallet's Doppleganger. You are getting the feel for how a big star was made. It's like being in an oil-painting class. You look at the works of Van Gogh and Rembrandt and you learn how they achieved their great canvases—how they mixed their paints, chose their subjects and so forth.

Then you go off and do your own thing. If you look around the bigtime TV scene you'll not see anyone who is a direct pinch of someone else. Michael Barrymore, for instance, first got noticed by doing a terrific Basil Fawlty take-off. When you see him work now he might still remind you a bit of Basil when he moves. But neither Basil Fawlty nor John Cleese host their own game show and variety show. On the subject of Cleese, Angus Deayton reminds me a lot of Big John, not only in looks but in manner of speech. I'm not suggesting for a minute that Deayton has copied Cleese, although I'm sure he, like most of the new generation of comedians and writers, will be a great admirer of the legendary Monty Pythoneer. And anyway, Deayton is his own man. Cleese has never hosted a show like Have I Got News For You, and is never likely to.

Vic Reeves and Bob Mortimer have never hidden their admiration for the late Eric Morecambe and his partner Ernie Wise. When Vic and Bob were growing up in the Sixties, Morecambe and Wise were their idols and inspiration. Vic now wears Eric Morecambe glasses but you'd never call it copying. I still prefer to think of Eric being inspirational to young Vic. And I'd argue that when Chris Evans finishes his Toothbrush show with the Morecambe and Wise song "Bring Me Sunshine" he is paying tribute to the great duo, not aping them.

I've taken Rowan Atkinson as a good example of a star to target if you are interested in comedy. But he's just one of a galaxy to choose from, covering every area from sport and news through to drama and action telly like The Gladiators. The process is exactly the same...watch, watch again, think, read about them.

And maybe even meet them. If there is a public appearance, like a supermarket opening, get down there and try to make contact. Don't be bashful. Become a superfan. Say "Gosh I've always wanted to meet you". Move in close and see what they are like in the flesh. If you are really cheeky you might even try the old nightclass number on them "Could I possibly interview you for my project/college magazine/nephew's scout troupe newsletter?".

If you do get to spend quality time with the star you have targetted, don't give any blatant clues...like the fact that you want to be a bigger star than them one day. You'll find advice very thin on the ground. In fact you'll note the air freezing over in dressing room. Talk only about them. That's the way they like it. And pick out certain points in their career you may have read about. They might be able to expand on some areas, and correct inaccuracies. There could even be admissions of wrong paths taken, or bad advice taken aboard and acted upon.

Also, have a little chuckle within. Tell yourself quietly that one day you are going to be sitting in a dressing room like this.

NOW YOU TRY

You have been watching Rowan Atkinson videos until your eyes feel like bleeding. Now it is your turn to have a go. You'll find it is not nearly as easy as it looks. But try you must, because before you go out there and start trying to crack the bigtime, you are going to have to put in a lot of practice at home.

Thank God for modern technology. The video recorder makes it possible for you to replay programmes or sections as often as you need. Then there's the camera, or camcorder which gives you the potential to make your own TV shows, even down to basic editing in some cases. What wonderful tools for the do-it-yourself television star.

So, down to work. Choose a particular sequence you really like. The beach scene for instance. Start replaying it over and over until you have learned the whole routine. You'll have to watch carefully, because what Rowan does with his trousers and swimming costume seems very much like conjuring. Now sit down somewhere quiet in your house and have a go yourself. Imagine you are there by the sea and there is another bather on a towel over to your right who might well be watching as you struggle to get your cossie on under your trousers.

Also, try and imagine an audience is watching you too, and hopefully will be amused by your antics. Bearing in mind that when Mr Bean is doing his stuff some twelve million viewers are looking in. But at this stage don't actually perform in front of any people. Your early practice sessions should be strictly behind closed doors. Why? Because if you are shy about your inexperience and your first tentative efforts, you might get the wrong sort of laughs, and be put off altogether. I'd hate for anyone to be tossing the book away at this stage. If you are confident, then you might go over the top and bid for the easy laughs, forgetting that you are supposed to be on a learning curve.

You are going to need help, but from people you trust who are really supportive, and who don't think you are crazy for having a shot at professional telly. As your practise sessions get more intense, these friends are going to be your crew. They'll work the camera, direct, help with the script, find props and locations. In fact you are setting up your own little production unit. It'll be fun for all of you.

Back to your battle with Bean, which at this stage is still happening behind closed doors. When you think you have it right, try the routine on your number one helper. Don't show them the original first. Just let them see your version and see if you get a laugh. Don't worry if there are no chuckles.

Now show the friend the authentic Atkinson tape. If he or she laughs at Bean and not at you, which is highly likely, ask where you are going wrong? If and when criticism comes, listen and take it in good spirit. Initially your efforts are going to seem quite amateurish.

Have another shot, taking your partner's comments aboard. You are now involving your helper as a kind of director. You have a difficult path to tread. On the one hand you need, and must listen to other people's opinions. But deep down you must follow your own instincts. In the end you will become a star in your own right out of self-belief and single-mindedness. You'll get nowhere if you are forever drifting this way and that, reacting to a whole lot of clashing advisors.

A note, too, about the use of the video in regard to your stardom trek. It's alright to record various performers to watch how they work, but remember this is only for general inspiration. Don't at any stage attempt to nick any material, or chunks of an act. You could end up in court. Artists go to a lot of trouble to protect their territory and you can understand why. Good ideas mean big money.

O.K., so you have gone as far as you can with Mr Bean in your back room. Now for the quantum leap. You are going on camera. If you haven't seen yourself on film or tape before it is probably going to be a shock. You won't believe you look that bad. And I'm afraid you probably do. Don't worry though. We'll be fixing all that later. You are going to need access to your own camcorder over the next few months. If you don't own one, hire a camera when you need it. They're fairly cheap to hire and reasonably straightforward to use. I'm not going to give long lists of where to rent one, and dedicate an extra chapter on how to use the bloody thing. That'll slow us up. Hit the local rental shop and do a bit of asking.

So far you have one friend or associate helping you. That's assuming you haven't had a giant punch-up in the back room when she said you were more like Mr Banana than Mr Bean. It's going to be useful if this person can use a camcorder. If not your production crew is going up by one extra person. So now you have camera operator, director, and you the star/producer. Exciting isn't it. Almost Hollywood.

You are now going to attempt to record your own version of the Mr Bean beach sequence. Let your cameraperson have several looks at the original, to note, for instance, how close to get to you during various bits, and whether the camera seems to be shooting from a high, low or medium aspect. Is the camera used to get a laugh? Does it suddenly swing away to the bather nearby, or focus up the seagull in the sky? It will probably be useful for someone to take a few notes, which will serve as a useful reminder once you get out there on location. Bear in mind that on the Mr Bean shoot there would have been a detailed script, even though Rowan speaks no lines during the sequence. The cameraman needs to know what the order of the action is.

Anyway, you should know a lot of this by now if you did as instructed earlier and got yourself friendly with someone in TV. You will begin to see how important it is to understand how a TV team is made up, and who does what. At this stage, if you can actually persuade someone to let you go out on a professional shoot—a drama, comedy, or even a commercial—it would be very useful for you. Go around the unit and ask everybody what they do. Take notes, learn, absorb information.

Meanwhile, back on your shoot, you have found a quiet field or back yard and it's action time. Your team is now four, because you've roped in a nonspeaking extra to play the other bather who lies silently on a towel nearby. The whole scene is funny because Mr Bean thinks the guy might see his naughty bits, and his attempts to stay modest while putting his costume on under his street clothes is the cause of all the weird body-bending. The fact that the man turns out to be blind is a wonderful tagline. But forget this when you are doing your version with your extra. For all intents and purposes he can see you. And under no circumstances can you afford to flash in front of him.

Have several goes at the sequence, listening all the time to your director and your camera operator, but still nonetheless doing what you think is right. A fine line to draw. You will realise why so many film and TV series end in tears, with all sorts of creative clashes. At this stage, anyway, try and keep it all good fun, and laugh off any skirmishes.

Take the tape home and look at it straight away. This is called "rushes" in the film game. After a day shooting on location everyone sits down that night and views the film that has been shot. Don't rush up to the bathroom and commit suicide straight away. This is your first attempt. Think of all those corny old sayings like having to be able walk before you run. In the cold light of dawn have another look. Was it really that bad? If it was, why? Get the rest of the team in. Hear them out. Get Rowan out again and look at how Mr Bean did it. Make specific note of how, and why you went off the rails. Then get out there and do the whole thing again...only this time on a real beach, as near as possible to the real thing.

If you are a real detective you might actually find out which seaside resort the Mr Bean unit used for the filming. You could finish up on the very same bit of beach Rowan used. What a buzz, Eh? I'll give you a helping hand if you want to tackle Mr Bean's famous picnic saga—you know, the one where the buzzing insect keeps diving on his sandwich. That was shot in Battersea Park, London, on a grassy knoll near the statue I call The Henry Moore Trio.

We've been covering comedy, but the same learning tricks and rules of practice apply to most other areas of on-camera activity—with the exception of acting. I've got a special chapter on that subject later. It's a question of looking carefully, watching how your chosen performer works, then having a shot yourself, no matter how clumsy and crass it might all seem when you first start. But then, didn't you wobble a bit when you first learned to ride a bike? You probably bounced off on your bum a few times. And here you are now, competing in the Tour De France.

Let's say you have your eye on Bruce Forsyth. You've been watching a fair bit of Generation Game and you note Bruce's ability to hold a big TV event together. You could well be intimidated. How the heck am I going to match that? The answer is that you are not...well, not straight away. You are going to pick up a few tips from an old Master, who has been hosting game shows for 30 years.

We're going back now to the Sunday Night at the London Palladium shows and Bruce's hilarious Beat The Clock game. What made it all so watchable was the way he treated the poor contestants. It was close to bullying. He would strut this way and that, chin sticking out, bossing them about the stage, haranguing them if they failed to understand something, or got the game wrong. "I'm in charge," he'd shout, and that of course became his catch phrase.

So, there were certain things about Bruce Forsyth that stood out then, and are still evident now. The jerky, rooster walk. The tendency to push people around, even bodies much bigger than him, and get away with it. The utterance which is immediately associated with him: I'm in Charge.

You're not going to copy Bruce. There's no point. He's already there. He'll beat you at being himself any day. Look carefully at yourself. Is there anything distinctive about how you move, how you deal with your friends and colleagues? Is there something you utter all the time, particularly when exasperated? When you can't find your car in the multi-level park, or your baby daughter has just peed over your CD collection, do you shout out "Stuff me like a Christmas Turkey"?

We're searching for things that can be developed, exploited and eventually turned into trademarks which your public will instantly recognise. More often than not these are mannerisms or sayings which are natural to the person. You can't manufacture them. I remember years ago when Michael Barrymore was rehearsing for the pilot episode of his new game show Strike It Lucky he had a writer who kept making suggestions for a catch phrase, but none seemed right. Michael had a habit of saying "Orwight?" when seeking approval, or talking to contestants. And that's the phrase that has stuck.

Maybe you don't immediately realise what is odd or different about you, and you're probably going to have to ask your loved ones. There could be some revelations. Like the fact that when you are walking and thinking at the same time you look like an Orang Utang doing Groucho Marx impersonations. Or when you are perplexed you stick your right finger in your ear and try to swallow your nose.

Then ask yourself this? Is there anyone presently on television who has an apelike Marx Brothers walk who puts a finger in his ear and swallows his nose when a contestant gets bolshy? Oh yes, and tends to cry out "Stuff me like a Christmas turkey" if anything goes wrong? There isn't? Good, then you are in with a fighting chance.

Later we'll be dealing in more depth about the various changes you might have to make in your appearance—clothes, make-up, hair and so forth. Also in some cases your voice. But these are all cosmetic. The Chris Evans hair and specs, the Paula Yates tattoo. The most important factor in stardom is the person inside all this. We have to concentrate on getting all the best personal qualities and talents out there on public display.

O.K., so you've clocked Brucie and The Generation game and you've sorted out a few of your own personal quirks. Now you want to have a go. Well, if you intended to stage your own Generation Game it would mean a lot more helpers than was required for the Mr Bean sequences. Also an elaborate television game involving so many people and so much movement is impossible to cover on one camera with an amateur operator. On the real Generation Game they have up to six cameras.

For the time being, don't bother with the camcorder. Get some experience in being ringmaster or host at a function where games are involved. An obvious and easy point is a kids' party. Organise the session, and have good games that will stimulate and excite the kids. Make sure you fully understand the games yourself, then when play starts, take charge, like Bruce. Instead of the camera, get your trusted helper/associate producer/director to watch how you have conducted yourself, and listen to the criticism later. Did you lose control of the situation at one stage? Did you fail to spot the potential in a little kid who was a bit of a character? What about the mannerisms? Did you do your ape walk? What about the finger in the ear? And did you at any stage ask to be stuffed like a Christmas turkey? You didn't? Well make sure you do next time.

Incidentally, don't think there is anything demeaning about making your start as a childrens' entertainer. Look at Noel Edmonds and his Multi Coloured Swap Shop. In fact one of the reasons Noel's House Party is so successful now is because Edmonds can appeal to a full family audience, kids and all. Then there's Phillip Schofield, who used to host kiddies' TV on BBC1 before he moved on to prime time. When Schofield was first getting started in the business he'd send videos of himself to producers and agents. It got him noticed. I'll be giving you tips on how to do this soon, but understand now the advantages of the camcorder.

As I was saying earlier, the use of the camera isn't advisable first up when you are learning to be a game show host. But further down the track, you can get someone to record you as you run a games night at the local scout troup, or something like that.

The results will be rough and ready but at least you will get some idea of how you are coming across, and whether or not you seem in control.

Using this look-learn-try formula there is scope for practise in so many areas. For instance, if it is a news reporter you want to be, then go somewhere interesting, attend an exciting function, then come back to your garden, stand in front of the shed and do a piece to camera saying exactly what you have seen. You don't need a helper even for this. Just stick the camcorder on a tripod or a chair and get cracking. If you've just been involved in a car crash (and are not hurt, obviously) or have seen a bank robbery or street punch-up, rush to that camera while the images are still vivid in your mind. Go for emotion and atmosphere and conjurer up scenes of drama with your words.

Likewise with a sporting event. If you've come back from a particularly good and exciting event—the cup final or the grand national—stand by the apple tree and tell the camera all about it.

Don't worry if the neighbours think you are bonkers. One night, when they turn on their telly and see you on the screen, they'll understand what all it was about.

INSIDE JOB...WHEEL IN THE TROJAN HORSE

Right at the beginning I talked about TV stars being walled up in their castles and how I'd drop the drawbridge to let you in on their secret little world. Well, the best way to get the bridge down and you inside is by the Trojan Horse method. Remember the story? Don't hold me exactly to the history books, but it goes something like this. A group of soldiers got inside a heavily guarded fortress hidden in the belly of a giant wooden horse. The invaders left the horse by the main door and the dumbos on the battlements thought it was a gift. They rolled back the gates, wheeled the horse in. And low and behold, a trap door opened up in the gee gee's rib cage, the warriors slid down a rope and conquered the castle.

The TV system is the castle, the defenders on the battlements are the performers who will rain boulders, arrows and molten tar down on your head if you turn up at the drawbridge and announce that you want to be a star like them. No, you have to be crafty. You go into the industry in a non-threatening job. That's your Trojan Horse. And once inside, you move stealthily towards the stardust jar.

We looked earlier at the case of Chris Evans, whose Trojan Horse was Timmy Mallett's mail bag. He took on the humble, low-key job of answering the star's fan letters. Imagine how far Chris would have got if he'd said to Mallett "I want to be a star, only a bigger one than you eventually. But in the meantime will you give me a few tips." He would have had a tip alright— over the edge of the nearest cliff.

Chris was smart enough to accept something menial to get himself past the door and into the system. We're talking basic infiltration here. Once you are inside you can see how things work. You'll learn who does what, and who are the powerful people you'll have to cultivate. It's a mistake to expect to go in too high up. The old ego could well be a bit puffed out by now. You've been doing a bit of starry stuff on the old camcorder, you've carried out some useful field research in the boozer with your Barrymore scene shifter mate or a make-up artist from Coronation Street, and you probably sense you need something important which should at the very least involve a door with your name painted on it.

No way. It could well be the tea urn to start with. Or a good pair of trainers to serve your feet as you run hither and thither as a messenger. Even this might not be as easy as you think. Television is a very glamorous business, and any sort of job connected with it, no matter how lowly, will always get snapped up quickly. The personal touch is very important here. That backed up with a bit of initiative. Your first move is towards the production team of a show or series you really like. The programme might be made by the television channel itself, or by an outside production company.

The clue is almost always found at the very end of the programme, when the final credits flash up on the screen. It'll say a BBC, LWT or Granada production, or mention another company—normally with an exotic or daft name like Giraffe, Bogroll or Extremely Upourselves—which made the show for the telecaster. Get on the blower to either the telecaster or the company or both and find out who does the hiring. Say you are very keen to get into television, you are not proud, you are very hard working and don't mind long hours and basically you will do anything.

Likelyhood is that you will be told that there is nothing doing just now, but put your details in the post and your letter will be kept on file in case anything should crop up in the future. Bullshit. It will go straight in the bin and you will be forgotten for ever. No, you have to get in there and see someone, make an impression. From now on people are going to being slamming doors in your face all the time. You've got to get into the habit of kicking them open again.

So, you'll almost certainly be told to put everything on paper. They'll probably call it a CV, short for Curriculum Vitae, the long-winded Latin name for your career record...or job sheet for plain talking people. Before they have chance to hang up on you, get in quick and say, yes fine but could you drop your details by in person and maybe just have a quick chat. It might just work. And if they do agree to meet you, you'll have the chance to shine.

A word of advice about the interview. Give the impression that you watch a lot of television, and if this is an independent production outfit, before you turn up make sure you have found out all the shows the company turns out.

Don't overdo things. Don't overdress or be too loud. Television people are usually very laid back and cynical. They've seen it all. They are used to dealing with real stars. Also, make your job sheet or CV very simple and truthful. Don't lie and say you've done show bizzy or telly things when you haven't. You'll get caught out.

But, if you have been keeping company with someone who works in TV as we've discussed earlier, don't be afraid to indicate in conversation that you do have some knowledge of the game. You might have heard about certain jobs which might suit you as you are climbing up towards the screen role. For instance production secretary, director's assistant, researcher. These are all good jobs which are medium range in importance—good positions to aim for once you have got your toe in the door with something very basic like teacup filler, messenger or receptionist. Say this is the sort of thing you'd eventually like to be. No harm done. You have reasonable ambitions and you know a bit about the trade.

A bit of reassurance here that working behind the scenes on a television production team can lead to a job in front of the cameras. Ulrika Jonsson was a secretary at TV-AM, the company which used to make breakfast telly, before someone got the bright idea of turning her into a weather girl. Jeremy Beadle, Jonathan Ross and Esther Rantzen were researchers. Look at them now.

One of the best Trojan Horse triumphs was pulled off by John Sullivan, who didn't finish up on camera, because that wasn't what he was after. He wanted to be a famous comedy writer and that's exactly what he is now. He's the guy who gives us Only Fools and Horses. John kept on sending scripts into the BBC and the commercial TV channels, and had collected enough rejection slips to paper a Jumbo jet hangar at Heathrow. He decided to fight the battle from inside the castle walls, and got over the drawbridge at the BBC Television Centre by getting a job as a scene shifter.

This won him access to the infamous BBC Club, a watering hole for all staff, from producers and directors to carpenters, stage hands and electricians. John did a bit of sensible asking around and drink-buying, and found out who were the powers on the comedy scene. He eventually zoned in on Dennis Main Wilson, a legendary producer whose credits included The Goons. John said he'd had a shot at a script and asked politely whether Main Wilson would mind having a quick flick through. His timing was lucky, because just at that time a directive had gone out amongst the comedy producers to look for and cultivate new talent.

DMW took the script home, loved it, got production under way immediately—and within seven weeks the first episode of Citizen Smith was being recorded at the BBC. John packed away his overalls, and has been busy at the pen ever since. He has also earned himself a nice little living and he deserves every quid. He wasn't put off, he didn't take no for an answer. He did it our way.

Getting on a production team gives you the golden

opportunity to be in the right place at the right time. It certainly worked for Jonathan Ross. He started out as a researcher. This job entails coming up with ideas and guests for shows, and preparing background notes for the host. Having been one myself I always found the job rather demeaning. A bit like being a butler.

In my Parkinson days I once told a journalist that researching for a big chat show was like holding someone's coat while they made love to stars. It got into print and caused a lot of amusement in the industry. But all the researchers knew what I meant. You get the big star, write all the questions, then you stand back and watch while someone else does the main thing.

Clearly, Ross wasn't going to hang around too long holding coats. He was too ambitious. He wanted the host's chair. And the host's money too of course...considerably more than a researcher's pay packet. A former colleague, who was a researcher at the same time as Ross, recalls how clever and subtle young Jonathan was in the way he made his move towards camera. "I remember we'd finished a series and were given a cash bonus of several hundred quid. I went off and blew my dough on a holiday, but Jonathan spent his on a really expensive designer suit. "He looked great, just great. And he knew it. Looking back now I realise he wanted to be seen as star material. He was already handsome and witty and a great hit with the girls. Not long after we were working again together getting up an idea for a new late night comedy chat show. No-one could think of a suitable host. Then someone said to Jonathan 'Hey, why don't you have a go?

"He didn't jump straight away. He was dead cool. He was non-committal. He said 'What, me? Oh, I don't know. Well, whaddja reckon.'

Then other people started saying it and Jonathan never actually said 'absolutely not'. The producer finally got hooked and Jonathan was given a screen test. He'd worked it like they were almost bullying him into it. Brilliant. And of course he gets the gig. Which is what he wanted all along."

The result was Last Resort, the late night show which was the making of Jonathan Ross. He is living proof that infiltration works. He got a job which gave him a useful background in the practical side of television, and he was around and in full view when someone was looking for a new TV star. Privately, although I have no proof, I would imagine he was practising like mad with his camcorder, or in the shaving mirror.

It was the same with Ulrika Jonsson. There was this lovely blonde girl sitting at a secretary's desk. Next thing she is in front of the weather map, and a new star is born. I am a great fan of Ulrika. She comes across as a complete natural. Well, like a secretary who has been turned into a star without going through that dreadful process that makes so many of our female presenters sound like hearty gym-mistresses who are addressing a lot of brain-damaged kids. It's like they were all trained on Blue Peter.

Esther Rantzen is another ex-researcher-turned-telly star. Like Jonathan Ross she made sure she was in the right place at the right time. She was a bright young thing on Bernard Braden's show some 25 years ago and managed to swing it so she did the odd consumer report on camera. Knowing Esther's reputation I would imagine she was a bit more pushy than Jonathan, and there's nothing wrong with that.

So the time came for change, and Esther finished up with her own show. Braden was shown the gate. Some say she knifed him. I say that is nonsense, a silly rumour born of jealousy. How would a young girl in a supporting role have that sort of clout with management? I'm not a great enthusiast of the Rantzen style of television. In fact it makes my flesh crawl. But I reckon she got That's Life because the brass were bored with Braden and wanted a new face on the box. Let's not take it from the woman. She did it our way too.

Other people have finished up switching from behind-camera to on-camera almost by accident, and claim to be genuinely surprised that they are now stars. Jeremy Beadle is one such case. Jeremy was one of the best researchers in the broadcasting business. He still is. His private library of reference books has to be seen to be believed. Two huge rooms full from ceiling to floor with books and files on every subject and oddity you care to name. If there was once a goat that famous for having two penises, Jeremy would be able to pick a book from his shelf and tell you when and where and what the goat's name was.

Jeremy assures me that when a producer had the bright idea of putting him in front of camera as one of the presenting team on Game For A Laugh, he couldn't understand why. "Well look at me," he said. "Do I look like TV star material?" It must also be said that the idea obviously caught on, because I haven't noticed Jeremy ignoring the cameras since. Fair enough. Put it down to happy discovery.

But, back to the beginnings. You've got to get your toe in the door first. And maybe pull a few stunts in the process. Let's paint the blackest possible picture. They've told you not to even bother putting the bloody CV in the post, and no, you can't call in.

Right, regroup. Plan another means of attack. Locate the office, hang around a bit, find out who delivers to the joint. Is there a sandwich service that calls around lunchtime? If so, approach the caterer and offer your services. Likewise with couriers. Often production companies will use just one messenger service. Get on yer bike.

What we are talking about here is darned cheek. You're going to need plenty of it as you make your way to the screen. Once you are past the receptionist and into the office, with the sarnies or the package you've delivered, get into conversation without being too pushy. If they get to like your style, it might occur to someone to give you a break as a runner, or even a cleaner. Don't hang back. Even suggest you do some work experience for nothing.

Television is all about personalities, and is fuelled by all sorts of weirdos and oddballs. If you say the right thing at the right time, or just be there when someone like you is needed, than bang—you're in. The wrong sort of thing would be to try and shoulder your way in as something outrageous—a hippopotamusgramme girl or a zany guy who delivers flowers on a unicycle—in the hope you'll make an impression. You'll make them throw up. As a raw beginner you'll rarely get wacky enough to impress hardened TV folk.

Much better to get in there nice and low key with something subtle. Better a fly on the wall than a braying donkey in the middle of the melee. Example: imagine a late-night session and the producer and writers are huddled around a table starved of ideas. You are there cleaning up, or have gone out for pizzas. Someone involves you in the conversation. They might try a gag out on you. Or an idea. You say, yeah, but could you not do it this way? Everyone laughs. The producer's eyes light up. Next day he takes you aside. Look, he says, no promises, but if you felt like slinging a few ideas his way on paper, he might well buy them from you. You do just that. And next thing, you've downed broom and picked up a word processor.

It can happen like that in television. One minute you have a brush in your hand, next thing you have taken one giant step towards becoming a TV star.

ALL CHANGE FOR THE STARLIGHT EXPRESS

Now's the time for some brutal self-questioning. If you were to go off to a studio today to host a top TV show would you be quite happy with the way you look, and sound? When that announcer off-screen trumpets your name, is it going to have the right ring? Is it starry enough? Are you starry enough?

The fact is that many celebrities working on TV today are very different from when they first started in the business. They have changed their voices, their names, their way of dressing. They have had hair grafted onto balding scalps, flesh carved from noses and bums and silicone injected into breasts. Often they have undergone inner change too, learning to be lethally tough on other people when they want their own way.

No need to book into the plastic surgeon or hair

transplant parlour just yet, or thumb through the yellow pages for a dialogue coach. In fact you don't have to make any snap decisions right now. Just be aware that something about you will probably have to change, or be radically modified as you prepare to board the starlight express. I have seen a picture of Paula Yates when she was about twelve, about to appear on childrens' TV in a cute little bunny outfit, complete with floppy ears. Half a dozen or so years later she had the punk hair, a tattoo on one arm and Bob Geldof on the other and was en route to notoriety and stardom.

This didn't happen by accident. Paula's planned it every inch of the way. The sex angle, for instance. When I first worked with her in the early eighties—on a Terry Wogan series believe it or not—she was a right little siren around the studio. She had a line of saucy chat which made even the most seasoned technicians blush. Her clothes were stylish but skimpy. When it came for the poor sound guy to wire her up, she would stow the power pack to her radio mike in her knickers, hoisting up her dress to tuck it away.

Of course stars have been changing their names since showbiz first began. There was often a good reason. John Wayne wouldn't have got very far as a hard man of film using his real first name—Marion. A few years back a young Irish comic called

Tynan O'Mahoney was finding work a bit thin on the ground when he first came to England. He figured he might do better if he moved up to the front of the alphabetical directory used to book funny folk, so he changed his name to Dave Allen. It worked a treat. More recently another comic, of Irish and South London pedigree, was working the comedy circuits as Paul Martin. One day he had a flash of inspiration, and changed his surname to that of his least favourite London suburb— Merton.

Neither Allen not Merton changed their voices. John Wayne didn't either. Having grown up with a girl's name he had already perfected a very threatening growl. These days there is nothing wrong with regional accents, bearing in mind once-upon-a-time you'd never get anywhere near a microphone at the BBC unless you had a ghastly, very plummy upper-class way of speaking. Even so, some stars have gone to a lot of trouble to sound posh. Sue Lawley, for instance. I'm told she once had quite distinct midlands twang.

The important thing is what you say and how you sound, not well-rounded vowels. Unusual delivery coupled with a local accent can have a lot of impact in the right circumstances. I remember as a kid listening to Radio Luxembourg—the only commercial broadcasting available in those days—when suddenly a weird babbling voice came over the air.

It sounded like a Yorkshire parking lot attendant on speed. This new disc jockey also addressed us as guys 'n gals and made very odd yodelling sounds. We were meeting Jimmy Savile for the first time, and hasn't he done well for himself without having to rely on speaking the Queen's English as per the text book. Once Jimmy had switched to television we realised he looked as bonkers as he sounded.

You're going to need more than the bathroom mirror to sort this one out. You should have had a camcorder pointed at yourself by this stage, doing your brother-of-Mr Bean routine, son-of-Bruce Forsyth or niece of Cilla Black. If you haven't you can no longer hide from reality. You've got to get some idea of how you look on a television screen. Let's assume that you do have something on tape. Play it back and ask yourself the very frank question: Are you really star material in your present style? Is anyone going to last a full five minutes without reaching for the channel changer? If you have any doubts, ask one of your helpers/friends or loved ones.

Take an overall view first without fretting over your hair or eyebrows or any other single detail. It's one thing to gasp in dismay when your holiday snaps come back from the chemist and there appears to be two of you squashed into one swim suit. Or you catch sight of yourself at your cousin's wedding reception, half-sloshed with your hand up a bridesmaid's gown, looking like a zombie from Michael Jackson's Thriller video.

If you look really bad on tapes you have made since you started reading this book then you need to think about change for the better. Generally, what is wrong? Are you right for the type of programme you want to host, or star in?

Do you seem lumbering, awkward, even embarrassed when running your game session? When you are interviewing the contestants do you cut in before they get a chance to answer properly?

More often than not, what is wrong can be righted—once you acknowledge it is wrong. Taking this wide, overall view of yourself you might realise you are falling down as a game show host because you are not good enough yet at people management. Note I say "yet" because you can always get better.

What's wrong then? Did you find out a little about each person before you started the game? Bruce is very hot on research when it comes to his Generation Game players. Was the problem the fact you weren't assertive or bossy enough with the contestants? Were you really in charge? Or did they run the game? In either case you can adapt. You change.

What about the clowning? If your Mr Bean on the beach didn't raise a single titter was it because you were too uptight? Did you really let yourself go? Were you trying to be too much like Rowan Atkinson and did that inhibit your style? Would you be better off having a go at your own routine, which you have devised yourself, with your own set of body contortions and facial gymnastics?

And the Kate Adie report you did from the coal shed—did that lack conviction? Did it come across as unintended comedy when you were supposed to be putting across an atmosphere of heavy drama? Maybe your subject matter wasn't serious enough. Weave a picture of horror in your mind. Imagine that you are first on the scene when an airliner has crashed into the side of a hill. You can see the rescuers pulling bodies from the wreckage. In fact you actually helped. You have blood on your shirt or blouse. Now do that bit to camera again with a bit of conviction.

Again this is change in the right direction. You are becoming a more serious reporter. A harder person. You are beginning to use your imagination, which is the broadcaster's best weapon.

If you are shrewd enough in your judgement of yourself, and what you have seen of your performance on videotape, you might decide on really radical change. You could be barking up the wrong tree. You don't really want to be a news reporter at all, do you. You're better suited to be a desk sergeant in

The Bill. You've decided on a job switch.

It's like the classic sequence in Monty Python's Flying Circus, where Michael Palin is the barber with the sharp razor who senses quite rightly that as a psychopath who hankers after cutting people's throats, he is not really suited to the job. "I didn't want to be a barber, I wanted to be a lumberjack" he wails—thus leading into one of the funniest song routines ever to come out of British television comedy.

If you past the main test, and you seem O.K. for your chosen role but something isn't quite right, then let's pay a little attention to detail. The pitch of the voice, maybe? A bit harsh on the lug 'oles? Not an uncommon problem. The Tory party spent big dollars getting Maggie Thatcher's voice down one octave and several hundred decibels quieter. You don't need to go out and remortgage the house for expensive elocution lessons. Use your own instincts to fathom out what sounds wrong. Then practise in private with an ordinary tape recorder, reading passages from book or magazine article, or just thinking aloud. Keep playing it back and keep re-recording. Imagine your voice as a lump of clay that you are modelling into something really special.

Chris Evans has gone for a very high pitch and rapid delivery, which—along with the specs and hair—are all part of the personality package. Far from losing her Liverpudlian lilt, Cilla has accentuated it. She's made a special feature of certain scouse words. I go to Liverpool regularly. I love the city. But I've never heard anyone say "lorra lorra" like she does. Vic Reeves and Bob Mortimer come from the North East and use their Geordie accents as comedy weapons. Stephen Fry on the other hand has the sort of strangulated upper class Cambridge delivery which seems oddly out of date...a throwback to the days when the vicar came for tea and Lavinia bounded in through the French windows to ask; "Anyone for tennis?". His speech hasn't held him back. If anything it is his trademark. So, if you are not ashamed of your accent and the area you hail from, and you can be understood without subtitles, my advice is...stay as you are.

What about body shape? I'm going to advise extreme caution and common sense here, because there is an epidemic of eating disorders at present, with healthy young girls starving themselves to look like Kate Moss, trying to shed the delicious natural curves nature has bestowed on them. I'd say, whatever you've got, be proud of it and flaunt it. Your friends and family love you for your personality, not your shape. It will be the same with your viewers once you are famous. If you are going to shed weight, do so because your doctor advises it for health reasons, not because you think it will make you look better on telly.

Make up your mind what size you are going to be before you become famous, because that's how the public will expect to see you. If Dawn French suddenly slimmed down to size ten I doubt whether she'd be as popular, or as funny. Likewise with Noel Edmonds. If he allowed himself to balloon out to sixteen stone his public would stop accepting invitations to his house parties. If you are going to trim down, do it by sensible exercise. For instance, if your beer belly or ample hips are spoiling the action when you are running your game show sessions, take up tennis or netball or a limb-loosening activity like yoga.

When it comes to other things like clothes and hair, there's no need to charge the gate straight away. Have a good look round and note stylish dressers you see when you are out and about. Scan the trendy magazines and clock what clobber the in-crowd have hanging off their backs. Also the cut of their hair.

Now plan your look. Aim for something a bit original or eccentric. It doesn't necessarily have to cost you a fortune. Courage is the key. Let's say, for instance, that you decide to grow an old-fashioned waxed moustache, or one big Clockwork Orange false eyelash and lipstick on only the top lip. You could set a trend. And note, too, I've suggested things that will show up easily on camera.

This changing process can be subtle and gradual, but sooner or later you are going to have to make your move, go public, and show that you are heading for the bright lights. The day Jonathan Ross went out and blew a small fortune on his first designer suit, he knew he was on his way to stardom. Oh yes, and he hadn't bothered to lose the speech impediment either. He probably figured that would help people remember him, along with the snazzy clothes.

Clever boy.

HIT THEM WITH IDEAS

Television is fuelled by ideas. The higher the octane of the ideas, the better the show performs. Bright ideas operate at all levels of the industry. Programmes themselves are created by ideas. In fact, if you devise a hit show like This Is Your Life or Blind Date and the format is sold all around the world you are likely to be a serious earner. As Cilla would say, you'll pull in a lorra lorra money.

If it takes one bright idea to invent a programme, then it takes thousands more to keep it on air. Telly is a greedy, spoilt, glittery creature which chomps through material at an alarming rate, burps loudly then wants even more. So, if you can come up with some bright ideas you are going to do well in the business...just so long as you make them work to your benefit and don't let anyone else steal them and claim the credit. I'm afraid this does happen.

We're going to look now at ways to use your ideas to get you into that star dressing room. You might be shaking your head and moaning "but I don't get ideas." I find that hard to believe. Everyone gets ideas, even if they are as simple as "let's go out and get a video and pick up a Chinese meal on the way home". You might even be getting ideas as you're sitting there in front of your set and not realising it. For instance, you could think, wouldn't it be great if The Bill did an episode about a crook who uses a hang glider to nick television aerials. That's an idea. If you were sitting in on a script conference at The Bill production office and brought this little gem up, you might get a pat on the back and see your idea a few weeks later on the screen. You might also get called a stupid tosser and told to shut up. There you go, win some, lose some. Telly's like that.

Put this theory to the test. Watch your favourite show, or an episode of your regular soap or crime series, and see if there isn't one area where you could have made some improvement—or added something you would have liked to have seen.

You might have liked to see Jeremy Beadle surprise a VAT man as he turns up for a routine check on a newly established company to find he has entered a fully equipped torture chamber staffed by whip-wielding ladies in black leather. You could, from the comfort of your sofa, invent a new contest for The Gladiators where the opponents have to swallow half-a-dozen hard boiled eggs each before seeing who is first to drag a double-decker bus up a steep ramp with one arm.

Now we have a rough idea what a TV idea is, we have to decide how best your clever wheezes can work for you. Well, if you haven't cracked a job on a production team yet, it could open the door for you. And if you are in but are doing nothing more challenging than polishing the photocopier and getting in the lunchtime fodder, then it could be your way to move up to a more creative role.

During my career I have had to hire—and fire—production staff. On first meeting it is so easy to separate the gems from the junk. I'll give you an example. For a couple of very tough years I was executive producer of Tonight Live in Australia. The show ran every night Monday through to Friday and offered a dangerous and often headline-making mixture of interviews, live stunts, oddball comedy and great music.

Five hours of live TV every week meant that we were always desperate for good ideas. And I was always on the look-out for good people to help me make the shows. I tended to interview would-be staff in the mornings. The rest of the day was too busy. My first question would always be "What did you think of last night's show?" If the answer was:"I didn't see it" then the next question from me was usually "Can you find your own way back to the lift?" How dumb not to watch the very show you are applying to work on when you are seeing the boss the next morning. You'd be surprised how many fell at the first fence. One or two even said they didn't watch the show at all, full stop. They normally didn't make it to the lift. I had them out of my window.

The encouraging candidates would have watched the show, and even better, when asked would have some constructive criticism about what they'd seen, and maybe not liked. I would then invite them to make suggestions about what they would have done to zap the show into life if they'd been involved. Often their medicine would have come in very useful on the night. If, under further questioning they had some ideas for future shows and started giving me some I could actually use, then I would be in serious hiring mood.

The lesson to learn from this is that there will always be someone somewhere in television who will be happy to know about you, and even offer you a job, if you can come up with suggestions which will help the programme. You have to aim your ideas sensibly, to the right target at the right time. No real point in shooting off absolutely blind. For instance, if you were to post off that story slant about the hang-gliding aerial burglar to The Bill production office without knowing anyone there, or anything about how the team works, then you would almost certainly be wasting your postage stamp.

But if you have been following my earlier advice about infiltration, and you are quietly socialising with a make-up artist or production assistant from The Bill, you'll know who to hit with your story idea. You might even get your eyeballs across an old script, and have a shot at your own episode.

I'm being careful to say old script—that is, one which has already been made and put to air—because at no point do I want you to break the law, or play foul in the TV game. I'm certainly not encouraging any Watergate raid on a production office where filing cabinets are rifled and future storylines or programme plans pillaged.

Don't pinch other people's ideas. Concentrate on developing your own. There is absolutely no harm in you flicking through an old script because you can get an idea of how to lay out your own words on paper, and this in turn will make life much easier for any producer you approach when you try and sell your work. But it would be totally wrong for you to lift another writer's material. Anyway you would soon get sussed, you would get a bad name and you will suffer as the result. The same rules apply here as to the process of star targetting, covered earlier. Look at someone's work, be inspired, but don't pinch.

Set out to be an original. Because that is the way you will eventually get to be a long-lasting and truly successful TV star. When you finally hit the nation's screens you are going to be fresh and original. You don't want a stale whiff of:"Ooo, ain't he a bit like Matthew Kelly?" Or: "Blimey, she wiggles her bum just like Anneka Rice when she runs."

So, back to the right strategy for lobbing in those ideas. Look for programmes that are on every day for a couple of hours or more and therefore obviously suck up huge amounts of material. Breakfast telly is a good example. Watch a particular channel for one whole week until you are totally familiar with the format, what happens regularly each morning, and what days the experts drop in. For instance, the vet on Monday, the skin expert on Tuesday, the astrologer on Thursday. And so forth.

Now, sit back and think to yourself—what's missing? Maybe they haven't covered home improvement—which might be your total obsession. In fact, if you have the sort of ego that is one day going to propel you to stardom, you will be convinced that there will be no-one in the country, in the world, in the universe, who can put up a shelf like you.

Your temptation might be to blast in there and suggest yourself as the person for the job. And who am I to try and stand in your way, because in this game Who Dares Wins, crazy things happen all the time. I am going to suggest caution though. You might have done a few things by now on your camcorder which will have convinced you that you are ready for screentime. What you have recorded almost certainly isn't as good as you think it is. And your work hasn't been judged by professionals yet.

So, put down on paper a couple of really bright and original home improvement ideas...building a cocktail bar out of an old wheelbarrow, or making a ceiling look like the roof of an ancient cave. If you are really confident of your performing ability, make your own cassette in which you are explaining how it is done. Now send both off to the show, having rung up beforehand to find out who is the right producer to approach. I'd advise dealing with producers rather than the presenters because your package will finish up in a fan-mail sack, might spend weeks being ignored, and might just end up in the right place—on a producer's desk. So take the short cut.

Your covering letter should say that you note there is no home improvement section on the show, and that you would love to help create one. Point out that you have expert knowledge of the subject and give the two examples you'd worked out. This is the smart line to take. Suggest you would like to write, research or come up with regular spots for the show. Then explain that you are enclosing a video to back up your paperwork, and illustrate how you think your two ideas might work.

At no point do you suggest you should present the sequence yourself on camera. Let them be the judge of that. If you have potential, and the wind is in the right direction that morning, you will impress someone and they will get you in for a chat. If your script and your tape are really brilliant and I were producing the show in question, I would get you in on one morning to do a single item to see how you shaped up under battle conditions. If the tape wasn't so brilliant but the ideas stood out proud, I'd have you in to the office for a bit of a chat to see whether I could use your creative juices on a professional basis.

A word of warning here, because as I hinted earlier, there are unscrupulous people in the business who will rip off your ideas. It would be a horrible and possibly terminal shock for you to be watching the morning show a few weeks later and see someone else doing building your bar in their front room and saying how clever they were to come up with such a wheeze. When you send the tape off to the programme, also send a copy of the covering letter to yourself. It will come back to you postmarked, and that is proof of when you submitted the idea. Also, when you make your tape, leave in shot a newspaper published that day, preferably with a very distinct front page picture and headline. Hang on to the paper. You now have further proof of when you committed your original idea to camera.

Letting them decide whether or not you are on-camera material is a sensible and subtle way to go about things. It's cool. Like Jonathan Ross hanging around in his smart suit, looking glam and saying "Oh, what me on camera?"

Mind you, I'm not suggesting for a minute that you roll over and die if you get the thumbs down on this attempt. There are many more shows on your screen, many more producers eager for ideas. Don't take me too literally about the home improvement angle incidentally. I haven't watched any breakfast TV recently. It's not my favourite entertainment. Maybe one of the shows already has a pet DIY performer.

The point I'm making is, look around and spot the gaps. Then make your move. I can't bang home this point hard enough. Never give up. There's nothing really easy about television. Challenges are going to be put your way the whole time, even when you are an established performer.

Meeting them head on, and beating them is what is going to make you, and keep you, a special star.

PLAY THE GAME

There are various ways members of the public finish up on television. One of the commonest is what we call in the business a 'Vox Pop'. This is short for another grand-sounding Latin phrase Vox Populi and means 'voice of the people'. In other words the camera will go out into the streets and ask you what you think of something or somebody.

Esther Rantzen was the best-known exponent of the Vox Pop in her old That's Life days. She usually seemed to be in possession of some odd vegetable which would appear to have grown a penis. She would thrust the lewd-looking mutant in front of a poor shopper's face and ask what it was. I always hoped the victim of this attack would scream back "it's a carrot with a willy you daft cow" but sadly that never happened. All sorts of programmes use the Vox Pop interview, from hard news and current affairs through to daily magazine and comedy shows. For the interviewee, it is a quick and fleeting flash of fame. Andy Warhol made the famous prediction that one day everyone will be famous for just fifteen minutes. The Vox Pop has cut this time limit down to ten seconds in some cases.

I was about to say that no-one becomes a lasting star out of the Vox Pop until I remembered one famous exception. What I am now about to tell you could only happen in Australia. It is truly the land of opportunity, certainly where telly is concerned. I got all my big breaks there as a poor old Pom who had met with nothing but closed doors here. A couple of chapters along the way I am going to explain just how valuable the Down Under connection can be across all aspects of television.

So, here's the tale of the one man in history who rose from the Vox Pop to became a successful fulltime television performer, and eventually a Hollywood megastar. In the early seventies there was this nightly behind-the-headlines type show called A Current Affair which went to air live on the Nine Network in Australia. A camera crew and reporter were out and about in Sydney collecting the public's view on an issue of the day. They decided to take a high-level diversion and climbed atop the harbour bridge to speak to a group of maintenance men.

One guy shone out above the rest. He was laid-back, naturally funny and very opinionated. He was so good the producer went back for another dose. And the workman was even funnier next time. He finished up being invited to the studio, where he was given a regular weekly spot. This in turn was so good Channel Nine gave him his own comedy series. We're talking of course about Paul Hogan, Mr Crocodile Dundee himself. The classic self-made star. But of course there was that huge element of luck. If the camera crew hadn't hit the bridge that day there would have been no opportunity for him to show off his natural talent. Paul has since told me that under normal circumstances it would never have occurred to him to go anywhere near a TV crew or studio.

Apart from Vox Pops, the next most common way for ordinary folk to finish up on telly is as a contestant on a game show. You tend to spend longer on the screen than if you are stopped outside Tesco and asked what you think of the Common Market banning the sale of Welsh pig bladders. You also get the chance to appear in a big, brightly lit TV studio, wear theatrical make-up and get to swop words and chuckles with Brucie, Cilla, Des, Bob and co. You are a star for a night rather than fifteen minutes. Well, a bit longer in the case of Blind Date. You'll come back on another show to tell what an appalling weekend you had in Amsterdam with the cross-eyed, bad-breathed partner you chose on your first appearance.

Looking back over the short history of television, the examples of game or quiz show contestants becoming stars in their own right are very thin on the ground. In the Sixties there was Monica Rose, a chirpy little South London sparrow who made such an impression as a competitor on Double Your Money the host, Hughie Green, gave her a fulltime job as his assistant. Hughie was a great showman, also a great pusher of new talent. At this time he had another hit show, Opportunity Knocks, which was a launch pad for a host of new stars.

The demise of the big TV talent quests, and indeed big hearted guys like Hughie, have robbed bright newcomers of a terrific chance to strut their stuff. It certainly worked for the likes of Lenny Henry and Victoria Wood and you can't help wondering how they would have grabbed a break these days.

There was the case, too, of Fred Housego, the brainy taxi driver who experienced a brief fling of fame after winning Mastermind. Whatever happened to him? Contestants are like gunfodder. They are dispensable items. Useful for one or two goes, then tossed away to make way for the next batch.

It needn't be like that. And I think it is the contestant who is to blame. They make the big mistake

of not following through on what is a golden opportunity. I'll explain why in a minute or two, but first I am going to give you the inside knowledge on how to get on a game show as a player.
I've gathered these tips from production staff who actually choose contestants for the big shows. And their main advice is, only apply for a show you are familiar with and actually enjoy watching. Also, you must like the host. If you finally get to meet him, or her, a little warmth won't go far astray.

First step is that you write in for an application form. Some shows actually encourage this, and give you a box number. If they don't, drop a note to the producer and you'll get the paperwork in the post. It is vitally importantly that you fill in the questionnaire properly. This is the first hurdle and you must clear it. Bear in mind you are not alone. Over fourteen hundred viewers apply to compete on The Generation Game each year. Some questionnaires have up to 40 general knowledge questions. Answer them all...and get everything right. There is no excuse for leaving any questions out or giving wrong replies. It's not as if you are in an examination room. You're at home with reference books to hand. Leave any questions out and they'll assume you're lazy, you're a dumbo, or both.

If you are asked to give interesting stories about yourself make sure they are good yarns. Bruce

Forsyth always tells his team "Give me people I can bounce off". He reads all the forms himself. This dates back to an unfortunate incident when a researcher on Play Your Cards Right missed a story on a questionnaire when a contestant gave a hilarious account of a car falling to bits as he drove it down the road.

You'll be asked to send in a photograph of yourself. I would advise strongly against false economies here. Don't nick up to the local do-it-yourself passport booth. Even the most photogenic people finish up looking like mass murderers or mentally impaired patients in these dangerous cubicles. The contestant researchers on one big TV game show have a rogue's gallery. This comprises a big board with a whole array of terrible pictures sent in with application forms. Almost without exception, these poor souls have ruined their chances and their reputations in a cheapo happy snap booth.

So, the smart thing to do is have some shots done by someone who can actually use a camera. It is means paying, then do so. This will be money well spent. Also, no silly grins, daft hats or attempts to be wacky. Your form will finish up in the bin, and your picture pinned up there on the rogue's galley. Make sure you look natural, nice, unassuming but quietly brilliant.

Oh yes, and for God's sake don't try and cheat.

People have been known to send in pictures of better looking friends or relatives. Mothers have submitted pictures of their daughters. Of course, you will get rumbled straight away as soon as you get to the interview or audition, which is the next stage of the process if they like your questionnaire.

You will be asked to turn up to a rehearsal room, and be warned, you will be watched like a hawk from the moment you walk in the door. TV people are tough. They take no risks. If one duff contestant makes it to the studio the show suffers and the researcher could be looking for another job by daybreak.

You will be chatted to in what appears to be a casual way, but all the time they will be thinking; How is this bit of meat going to make out on the show? At least one big game show production company has a series of questions drawn up by a psychologist.

They will expect you to be nervous. Most people are. But if you are shaking visibly, vomiting everywhere or are incontinent, they will judge that you are probably a bit too highly strung for the telly business. Don't whatever you do take any drink or medication. You might overdo it, and appear too laid back or downright drunk.

Fear is an inevitable symptom of showbusiness, so don't worry. Even the most seasoned performers gets a bit skittish before doing their bit. Mike

Parkinson says that one thing he doesn't miss since giving up the bigtime chat show business is hearing the sounds of his guests throwing up in the next door dressing room as they suffer pre-show nerves.

During this audition you will be asked to play the game. The host almost certainly won't be present. There will be a stand-in who will be as near as dammit to the real thing. This is the point where you are going to look silly if you are not familiar with the show and don't know the rules. So make sure you have done your homework. During the practice runs, don't be a smart-arse. Don't be over-competitive and too quick on the buzzer. You'll be dropped sure as eggs is eggs. One clever dick is enough to unbalance a whole show. The other competitors get unduly intimidated.

If you come through the audition and are invited to be a contestant at an actual recording of the show, don't assume you are home and hosed yet. You have to meet the host. This will happen during studio rehearsals. I mentioned earlier it is important you like the star. If you don't, it will come through loud and clear in your performance, you will be politely asked to leave the station, and another contestant will take your place. Yes, they have 'spares' ready and waiting just in case this very thing happens.

So, let's assume everything has gone swimmingly well, you've appeared on your game show, and you came across as a right little star. What happens next? Well, maybe that's all you wanted. This book is designed to help you get on TV and if you are happy with one quick flurry of glory, that's fine. Maybe you want to become a regular game show contestant. There are some people who are so good at it they get to appear on dozens, sometimes all over the world.

I suspect, though, that if you have read this far you will want to be a star in your own right. If game shows are your interest, then you'll want to host your own. You do? Right, let's go on the attack. Positive action is what is required. Example: not so long ago there was a contestant who really shone when she appeared on The Generation Game in a mock auction. Her name was Kim Hughes and Bruce gave her the task of doing a sales spiel for a car..."The Forsyth Flier". She was great, very impressive. Star potential.

What has happened to her since? Nothing, as far as I gather. She certainly didn't land a regular job on telly. Why? Presumably because Kim was waiting for someone to make her an offer. It rarely if ever works like that these days.

You have to make things happen yourself. If you come across that well on a major game show, you grab hold of a video cassette of your marvellous moments and you show it around. You sell yourself. You look at various programmes which might need a bright new personality like you and you bang on the producer's door. Back this up with a new idea. Remember we were talking earlier about pestering a breakfast show with a new home improvement segment or something similar. Well, this strengthens your arm, garnishes your sales pitch. Still record your own clever segment...and have edited on to it the excerpt with you being outrageously witty and wonderful on Bob's Full House, Strike It Lucky, Generation Game or whatever.

You've got to convince producers that your game show appearance wasn't just a flash in the pan. What you're saying is, try this juicy red apple...I've a whole orchard of the same just waiting to be picked.

MAKE 'EM LAUGH

When I was a kid I had a wonderful teacher called Father McGowan. We called him Jock and he made mathematics easy at a time when sums meant suffering. How? Because Jock used jokes. We fell about laughing during his classes, which was a pleasant change from the tactics of his Jesuit colleagues, most of whom used to put their lessons across with a leather paddle. And the joy of Jock's way was the fact we actually learned maths, and passed our exams with no fear or effort.

I've always loved comedians. Not just because of Jock McGowan. As a toddler I used to have my ear clued to our old wooden radio set, particularly when the funny shows were on. At five I could do a passable impersonation of Frankie Howerd. My teen years were made magic by the company of Eccles, Bluebottle, Colonel Bloodnock and the rest of The Goons.

Then telly started stealing the big audiences from steam radio, and while many comics failed to make the transition from sound to vision, others like Tony Hancock flourished. Hancock loved the camera and it loved him back. He'd use his sad spaniel face as a laughter weapon. One poignant twitch of an eyebrow could be worth more than a dozen spoken gags.

Another radio comic to survive the coming of TV and actually thrive on the box was Bob Monkhouse. Boyish Bob knew how to use his face too. In the late fifties and early sixties, he was as big in television comedy as Rowan Atkinson is now. But then telly made its own brand new comedy stars like Bruce Forsyth. Bruce had to be seen to be laughed at as he pranced around the Palladium stage of a Sunday night, chin jutting out, and bossing about the contestants in Beat The Clock.

It's interesting to note that Bob and Bruce are still top-draw TV acts now, nearly forty years on. Why? Because they are funny. Which brings me to the point of why all this is relevant to you and your plans to be a TV star. If you have funny bones in your body, then you are best built to get where you want. You have a head start over everyone else.

Comedians have it made. They crop up everywhere. They get to work together in teams...Monty Python, Not The Nine O'Clock News, The Mary

Whitehouse Experience. They get to work in pairs...Mel and Griff, Vic and Bob, French and Saunders. They get to work solo...Lenny Henry, Victoria Wood, Rowan Atkinson. They get to work on their own and lead teams on sparky quiz shows like Have I Got News for You....Paul Merton.

They get their own variety shows...Des O'Connor, Michael Barrymore, Brian Conley. They get their own chat show...Jimmy Tarbuck. They even get their own straight drama series...Robbie Coltrane as the psychologist in Cracker. They get to travel the world making interesting documentaries...hello there, Michael Palin. They get cooking shows, motoring shows, any other show you care to mention. Yes, even the God Spot...Lord Love us, with Harry Secombe on The Highway. And of course they get to host most of the big game shows...come in Bob, Bruce, Des, Jim and co.

So you've probably got the drift by now. Get the laughs and you get the breaks. A sense of humour is important in all aspects of life, from work and play through to marriage and other personal relationships. The ability to make people laugh, and see the funny side of things, will certainly help you across most areas of television, not only in your bid to get on camera but in your dealings with colleagues on production teams.

Developing your sense of humour will help you

develop your identity as a performer. If you tend to amuse people it will often be because of a particular mannerism or habit. They'll sometimes even tell you "It really cracks me up the way you talk about traffic wardens as if they are evil robots". Or "No matter what clothes you wear, they never seem to fit your body". It might be the way you scramble up your words when you are agitated.

All these quirks, when identified, can be turned into trademarks. When Billy Connolly first started working as a comic up in Scotland he sported a pair of outrageous yellow wellies. The late and much-missed Les Dawson used to swallow his nose in mock anguish. Julian Clary began his telly career as a bizarre act called The Joan Collins Fan Club, working in tight spangly trousers and blouse and accompanied by a performing dog.

This all ties in with what we discussed earlier in the book, about looking for a particular catch-phrase. For instance, shouting "stuff me like a Christmas turkey" when your game show contestants are getting out of hand. Or a distinctive or original way of dressing. You are looking for ways to get noticed and remembered, and not merely by shock value...like dyeing you hair green and ripping all your teeth out.

We are looking at all options, all reasonable routes to get you on camera. It might be that when you've read this far you've realised you have always wanted to be a stand-up comic. The subject of how to become a comedian is a book in itself, but there are various simple guidelines you can follow now to put you on the right track.

Firstly you need to look and listen and familiarise yourself with all the main contenders on the comedy scene. This isn't quite the same as star targetting, as explained already. You are taking a broad sweep, not just focussing on one particular star you admire and want to learn from. You will see that each comic has a distinct style which separates him or her from the competition. If a couple of acts are too similar, then one will wither on the vine.

Take Dave Allen as an example. Even before he speaks there is that wild main of hair, the flashing eyes and of course the missing finger tip. He starts bellowing in that rich Irish accent. Only room for one sound like that on the bigtime comedy scene. Then there is Dave's subject matter. Nuns, priests, devils, religion in general. He also rants at all those rude, dozy and unhelpful people we all hate...doctor's receptionists, airline cabin staff, shop assistants, income tax inspectors and TV repairers. Other comics might hit these targets too, but not in such an angry way.

As far as distinctive accents are concerned, there's no mystery about where Billy Connolly comes from.

His Scottishness is all part of the fun, as are those wonderful stories about his early days in Glasgow. He has this marvellous gift of making you identify with what he is talking about—whether it is childhood, work, holidays, horrible people and life in general. He also has the best line in toilet talk and worse, and gets away with it out of sheer cheeky charm. Few entertainers can bring the house down simply by uttering the word 'willy'. And who else but Connolly would dare do a whole routine on telly about incontinence trousers?

Comics with strong regional accents tend to have personalities which are in keeping with the area they come from. Jimmy Tarbuck is a typical Liverpudlian. Brash, arrogant, cruelly perceptive. He'll call a spade a spade, then hit you over the head with it. Cilla is typical of the town, too, only she offers a little more loving warmth than old Tarby. Mind you, everyone's a comic in Liverpool. Every time I get into a taxi up there in Scouseland I get instant cabaret from the driver. The monologue will cover all subjects under the sun, from politicians to pop music. And of course they all knew a Beatle, or narrowly missed out on being one.

Jasper Carrott comes across as a rather morbid midlander. I imagine going into a funeral parlour in Birmingham and seeing him behind the counter, droning on in that flat voice about how all the cheap wood being used in coffin-making these days is causing an outbreak of casket-warp. Enough to make a corpse complain. Jack Dee is a deadpan act, too, only from further south. With his snappy suits and short hairstyle he reminds me of the young plain-clothed policemen I'd drink with when I was a reporter in North London. Either that or a villain from the same area. I often found it hard to tell them apart.

Paul Merton is another London comic who is very typical of his area. He often hosts his TV shows from a set designed to look like a sales kiosk in one of those rundown tube stations like Balham or Clapham South. He doesn't look out of place one bit. Paul also has wonderful flights of fantasy which reveal that he is part Irish. He made his name in the London comedy clubs with routines like the copper giving evidence in court while under the influence of L.S.D. He has an extraordinary obsession with dolphins. You'll see them crop up in various sketches for no sane reason.

So, we have taken a quick cross section of some famous laughmakers and identified what is special about them. Their look, their sound, their style, the region they come from. The more distinctive you are, the less likely you are to have people paddling in your pond. There is, and could only be one Alexei Sayle, with the suits three sizes too small, the Mussolini scowl and the haircut that looks like it was done with a sanding machine. No-one else could get away with reciting those potty poems like Pam Ayres, certainly not in such a fruity country-yokel voice. With Ken Dodd it's the shock of gravity-defying hair, the rabbit teeth, gob-stopper eyes and tickling stick.

All these stars had to start somewhere, so be reassured, not intimidated. A positive approach is vital here. You don't think "Oh God they are so good, I'll never be like that, I'm giving up here and now". You square up to the challenge and say: "They've made their mark in a particular sort of way, so shall I". And that is the secret. Ask yourself, what is missing from our screens? What's the gap in the comedy scene and how can I fill it? Again, don't expect a television station to offer you your own laughter show tomorrow. Paint a portrait in your mind's eye of the comic you would like to be, and plant that ahead of you as a target.

For absolute starters you are going to need some practice. You must face a group of people, preferably bodies you don't know, and you are going to try and make them laugh. All sorts of possibilities here. Join a local debating club. This provides excellent training in speaking your thoughts out loud. Most subjects you'll have to spout steam on will lend themselves to a bit of levity. So always aim to make your speeches funny where possible.

An important point—always try and make your humour original. Don't lace your act with tired old jokes. Dr. Jonathan Miller once described the joke as being like a clockwork toy...a humorous machine anyone can wind up and set loose, even if they don't have a sense of humour.

Thinking up funny material isn't easy. In fact it is bloody difficult. That's why professional comedy writers are such tortured souls. If you see a group of people who work on an entertainment show and want to find the comedy writers, head for the saddest faces with the deeply ingrained worry lines. One fairly easy route is telling stories against yourself. About the sod of a day you have been enduring. How you put your ballroom dancing club membership card in the bank machine by mistake. This might have really happened. But then you add the fantasy twist: "instead of getting cash out, I got sequins". Not exactly Morecombe and Wise, but it might get a laugh.

Let your imagination flow. O.K., so you hold a supermarket queue up for ages because you have chosen an unpriced item and an assistant has to go back down the aisle in question and check. That's what really happened. By the time you come to tell the story to your gathering it was the only product in the entire store without a barcode and it took ten people to sort it out. Meanwhile the queue behind you is getting angrier and death threats are being muttered. When the price is finally checked you find you don't have enough cash with you and have to leave the item at the check-out.

Brilliant comics like Dave Allen keep their material fresh by constantly drawing on real life experiences. In his case it tends more towards real life frustrations. Like dealing with unhelpful bureaucrats, airline staff and shop assistants. Dave's attempts to have his son's faulty sound-system changed at the big London department store where it was originally purchased had him almost frothing with anger when he told me about it shortly afterwards. A few months later it came over as wonderful comedy during his stage act.

Dave also has a morbid fear of lifts, dating back to a truly scary experience when he got trapped in one for several hours. When Dave is on the road he'll choose a hotel where he can have a room on a lower floor which can be reached by a staircase. This doesn't stop him getting fun out of the subject during his routine. He tells this true story about one occasion where, despite his protestations, he had to use a lift. It went up, then stopped. The door didn't open. Almost immediately he started hammering on the door. screaming and shouting to be released. There was a sound behind. A group of people were staring at him in wonder from the landing. It was a double-doored lift. He'd had his back to the one which had opened for that particular floor.

So, keep your eyes and ears open, and maybe even turn your misfortunes into comedy gems. The set out to find your audience. Of course there are ways to cut your teeth before playing The Albert Hall. You can offer to make a speech at your friend's big birthday party or hen's night. If there is a social club at your work, suggest giving a little talk on a pet subject. It might be to do with the frustrations of operating in your particular department, thereby giving you the opportunity to poke some fun at your colleagues. And the boss if he/she isn't there.

The thought of doing this might make you physically sick with nerves. Press on regardless. Terrify yourself. That fear won't necessarily go when you turn professional. In fact it will probably get worse. Knee-knocking goes with the job. But in compensation, you'll feel terrific once you get that first laugh. The adrenaline kicks in, and you are getting the biggest buzz around. Comedians will always tell you there is no greater high than causing a whole auditorium to rock with laughter.

Once you've grown confident on the first rung of the laughter ladder, seek out your local comedy venues and find out if and when they have open nights when beginners can have a go. This is the route Paul Merton took. Get yourself a good, tight little routine ready. Make sure you know it really well. Don't ever make the really dangerous mistake of thinking you can get up there in front of the crowd and something hilariously funny will suddenly come into your head. It doesn't work that way. All the best comics are well prepared, even if they appear to be making it up as they go along.

It can help if you do something else other than just stand there talking. Like magic for instance. Bad magic. I'm particularly partial to bad magicians. I was up there in the front row of the Tommy Cooper fan club. I've spent many happy hours in TV studios, theatres and clubs laughing at comedians, but I don't think I've ever hooted as much as I did one wet afternoon at a matinee in Scarborough where Tommy blundered around the stage of the Wintergardens theatre in that crazy red fez, getting six different conjuring tricks all hopelessly cocked up simultaneously.

Steve Martin started in showbusiness as a magician, too. He wasn't a bad conjurer —he was mad! I had the good fortune to work with Steve on his first-ever British TV appearance. The climax of his act was a round of cat-juggling, where he apparently whirled a litter of real kittens in the air. Without blowing the gag I'll just say that there was at least one live pussycat which never got hurt and a lot of very realistic fluffy models. But word got round during our rehearsals at the BBC and suddenly an R.S.P.C.A. man turned up. He took a lot of convincing that no dire deeds were being done to moggies, even when Steve did the juggle for him. What a shame we couldn't have put to air Steve's dialogue with the flustered official. It was almost as funny as the act itself.

That's magic. But there are other diversions. You might like to experiment with ventriloquism and come up with a really unlikely doll as a stage partner. And as you are a comedian, it doesn't matter if your mouth moves. In fact you might even dare to be different and do an act where your mouth moves and the doll's doesn't.

All this is fine if you want to be a stand-up comic. But there are other ways to use humour in your quest for on-camera fame without actually having to set yourself up in direct competition with Ben Elton, Paul Merton or Jack Dee. In your letters to producers, give the odd clue that you can see the lighter side of things. When you prepare your videos, introduce an original idea which could well produce a titter or too. Also, if you have got into the habit of thinking up material for yourself, it will be a big help if and when you get to host your first show.

Presenters break down into two main categories. There are those with little imagination who only work from scripts and rely on autocue...a remote controlled prompting system which projects words on a big screen across the camera lens. Then there are those who use autocue only as a general back-up, but can think on their feet and react to whatever is going on, bouncing off their guests and spinning natural wit and conversation.

These are the true TV performers, the ones who last the longest, the ones who become proper stars. This is the category I have set aside for you

IN THE SOAP....AND THE CONFESSIONS OF MISS X

The people who work on them prefer to call them 'dramatic serials', but to the rest of the free world they are 'soaps'. Short for soap opera, a term dating back to the big American radio serials of pre-TV days which used to be sponsored by detergent companies.

Soaps, then and now, pull in huge audiences. When the twenty top-rating TV shows are announced each week, the first five places are almost always taken by the big soaps Coronation Street and EastEnders. We are talking audiences averaging up to sixteen million viewers for the number one spot. Lower down the charts you get soaps like Neighbours and Emmerdale, and popular series like The Bill, Casualty and London's Burning. The difference between soaps and series, just for the record, is that soaps have a continuing storyline and series have self-contained stories.

The conclusion we draw from all this is the fact that if you get into popular drama on television you are going to play to huge audiences and you are going to be very well known. You are also going to have to be an actor/actress and I must draw a deep breath and admit that actors and actresses are my least favourite people in showbusiness.

Guess who said this? "Acting is an empty and useless profession—an actor is a guy who, if you ain't talking about him he ain't listening". I'll tell you who said it...Marlon Brando did. He's an actor himself, only he doesn't do much these days. With that low opinion of his trade you can understand why
At the time of writing this chapter Hugh Grant is the hunk, spunk he-man heartthrob actor of the moment thanks to two hit movies—Sirens and Four Weddings and a Funeral. A colour magazine has fallen out of one of my weekend newspapers with his smirking, smug face on the cover. His shirt is open to his navel and he is telling us: Aren't I just gorgeous?

The article backs this up. I only get to the third paragraph where Grant talks about not being able to pass a mirror or shop window without looking admiringly at his reflection and I can stand it no more. I fling the magazine on the ground. After years in the business, writing about actors, working as their publicity agent, researching them for the big TV chat shows, I know this type so well. No ill will intended to Mr Grant. He can't help himself. But he should be warned that in a few months, probably by the time this book is published, he will probably be forgotten and a new Mr Hunky Spunky will be all the rage. So enjoy it while you can, Hugh.

My opening encounter with the amazing vanity of the bigtime actor was in the Sixties when, as a boy reporter on a local paper I got to meet my first Hollywood star in the flesh. It was Laurence Harvey and he came to open a big new car showroom in our neighbourhood. All the time I was talking to him, Harvey was looking over my shoulder to something beyond. Occasionally he smiled, and flicked the quiff of hair that fell down his forehead. I assumed he was eyeing someone else across the room. A pretty girl maybe. I turned round. There was nobody else behind us, just a mirror. He was flirting with his own reflection.

If you are actor/actress material you will have seen nothing at all wrong with all this excessive self-love, and you will be angry about how cruel and cynical I have been about poor old Hugh. Worry not, read on, because this chapter is all about you, and my advice about getting you a part in a big soapie.

The wise words come not without difficulty. I said in the introduction how unlikely it would have been to have any big TV star reveal the true secrets of getting to the top— their reluctance being, of course, a defence. Well the soap opera crowd are a really closed shop. Their little world is not a walled city so much as a bunker reinforced to withstand a nuclear attack.

The key people in the soapie trade are the casting directors, certainly as far as your on-camera career is concerned. Their power is extraordinary, but so simple in operation. When the producers and script editors have come up with a new character the casting director will make the necessary suggestion as to which actor or actress is suitable. This is wonderful news for the lucky person, particularly if he or she has been out of work or 'resting' for a while, which is fairly common. This means months, even years of regular money and exposure to big audiences. It also means lucrative spin-offs like TV commercials, fete openings, and the sale of I'm-a-bonkaholic stories to tabloid newspapers. If the chosen one has never acted on television before then it is even more magical and wonderful. There suddenly is the storybook world of the dressing room, the bright lights, the costume-fittings, the thrill of seeing oneself on screen for the very first time, then getting recognised in the local supermarket.

All this at the whim of a casting director, but how will he or she have arrived at the crucial decision? The obvious assumption is that they flick open the various volumes of Spotlight, the showbusiness bible with thousands of actor/actress photos. Under each portrait are details of agents, body measurements and other thrilling personal details like: Cedric does scubadiving and Latin American ballroom dancing, and Janine speaks French and Icelandic and is a skilled horsewoman and rollerblader.

But there's a lot more to casting popular drama than thumbing through Spotlight, as I discovered when one of TV's top casting directors agreed to give me inside knowledge of the process, not only of selection, but on what was the best way to go about learning the trade and getting yourself noticed by powerful people like her. My "mole" understandably prefers to remain anonymous so in the true tradition of an old newspaper man I shall call her Miss X.

The first big powerful message to come across from Miss X was that you have got to go out and actually learn to act. You might think you can act, but if you were put to the test at an audition you would almost certainly come unstuck. It is much harder than it seems. Television drama is a tough business, and casting directors will only suggest people they feel could do the job. Just as anyone who runs a transport company will favour drivers who have the proper H.G.V licence.

How you get this experience depends on a lot of things...your age, your financial circumstances, how much time you have on your hands. And, of course, how keen you are to succeed. In an ideal world you would go off to The Royal Academy of Dramatic Art for several years on a full time course and graduate as the fully fledged item. But the world isn't always ideal. Don't we just know it. There is always a big rush on RADA places, and only a tiny proportion of the candidates get in. They are usually brilliant 18-year-olds with a basket of great exam results who have been spouting Shakespeare since they were toddlers. There are other colleges and learning establishments around the country in places like Manchester and Bristol which offer great fulltime drama courses, but again the demand for places is heavy, and the competition cut-throat.

But, as you will know by now, this is not a book for defeatists. There are other ways to learn acting, and you don't have to give up your day job, which is good news if you have a home and a batch of kids to support. What you do is to go out and join a local drama group and get your first experience at speaking lines. The amateur acting possibilities available to you will depend a lot on the area where you live, whether it is a big city or a small town.

Your choices could range from the village hall players, where the vicar is producer, director and leading man, to a more sophisticated drama workshop where members get to work alongside professional actors and are encouraged to write their own plays.

The answer is to get in anywhere. Don't be proud. Even in the humblest of local drama circles there will probably be an audition process, and possibly a long waiting list of would-be members. A word of advice here. When you go along for your interview/audition/exploratory chat, don't start blabbing about how one day you are going to be a big TV star. Most of the people in the group won't have your grand ambitions. They'll think that you are a horrible big head who will head straight for the juiciest roles and is only using the company as a stepping stone.

Which is true of course, but no need for them to know at this stage. Be keen but low key. Yes, of course you will be happy to accept walk-on parts with no dialogue as starters. And no worries about helping build the scenery, stitch up a few costumes, help with the tea and fairy cakes at the interval. Sooner or later, you will get your chance. You will have a few words to say, if only as the village policeman who puts his head through the window of Rose Cottage and says "excuse me Madame, but do you know you have left your car lights on?" You will be so proud of this one line you will think you are Anthony Bloody Hopkins, and you'll probably insist all your family and mates come along to witness the Oscar-winning standard of your performance.

And so you climb from there. You stay with the group until you have progressed to more important roles—a leading part at least. Then you look around for a better company. By this stage you'll be in on the local drama scene and you'll know what is available. If you are in a major city, there will certainly be amateur or semi-professional groups at various standards. Once you have some sound experience on the stage, be ambitious. Aim for the group you know to be the best, particularly if it has turned out performers who are now fully-pro and prancing around on telly screens and the West End stage.

Also, take aboard as much extra training as you can find. Lots of the adult education courses include evening classes in drama. Toddle along and see if there is anything extra in the way of tuition and experience. You might also hear that a professional actor or actresses gives private tuition. If you can afford it, try a couple of lessons. Get friendly with your teacher. You could finish up going to a few show biz parties, and rub shoulders with influential people.

Because your next move, says Miss X, is to get

noticed by people like her, the all-important casting directors. Miss X and co are always on the prowl, looking for new and unusual talent. They don't just sit at their desks thumbing through Spotlight albums. They tend to slide in quietly and unannounced when they hear that a drama group has a good production in progress, with an outstanding newcomer. That could be you. This isn't always left to chance. There are ways, explains Miss X, whereby you can drop the hint. If you are absolutely sure you are brilliant in the play and are prepared to be assessed on your performance with a view to possible TV work, then let the casting people know about it.

Miss X tells me she and her colleagues don't mind the direct approach. If the pitch is done in the right sort of way, it can serve as a sort of mini-audition in itself. Let's say that you have never done any telly before. Write in, not as yourself but as your mother. She is apparently raving on about how terrific her offspring is in this wonderful evening of entertainment. Then drop a few clues which suggest that the letter might not be genuine. "His father and I were so glad when he finally got into a theatre group...we were worried about him strutting around his house dressed like Henry VIII, trying to lop his wife's head off with the bread knife."

You have to stand out from the crowd, get yourself noticed. If you make the casting director smile a little in your letter, and enclose a good review from the local press, you could well get a visit at your playhouse a few nights later. Once you've clocked up one or two telly appearances, you should collect them on a cassette, which serves as your "showreel"...it shows what you have done to date. Have it edited together properly, and get several copies made. They tend to get lost easily. "The way showreels are presented to us is important," says Miss X. "One actor sends a tea-bag with his. He says 'put your feet up, have a nice cuppa and look at this'. Another chap sends me holiday photos of him, his wife and kids. It's a sort of blackmail, and it works".

Important tip here from Miss X. If you haven't done any telly yet, don't go off and make your own video. This might be OK elsewhere, when you are trying for a spot on a magazine programme or wacky entertainment show, as we've already discussed. But with acting it is different. They don't want to see you taking off Emma Thompson or Kenneth Brannagh by your garden shed. They want to see evidence that you've actually acted on screen.

Big question: how do you find the casting directors? Answer: use your initiative. I've already said this is not a book of lists. Get off your bum and on the phone. Ring the production companies who make the various soaps and series you would like to work on, say you are an actor or actress who would like to be considered for a part, and more often than not you will be given details of the casting office. As you start getting replies you'll gather names.

There are shortcuts. In some of the bigger cities there are organisations which will help you showcase your talent to casting directors...at a price of course. You pay an audition fee of around ten pounds, and if you pass this you have a week of workshopping each evening, at around the twenty quid mark. By the week's end there is a performance night when the major casting directors are invited along to see you strut your stuff.

"They really work," says Miss X "I've been along and spotted some interesting new talent." Two of the main London companies which do this are The Casting Couch and Mass Productions, but if you enquire locally you'll find similar organisations. If you are already in a drama circle you will probably hear about them anyway.

Any point in contacting your favourite soapie and trying to suggest yourself for a part you've created yourself? "There's no way of knowing," says Miss X. "New characters tend to be developed within the system, because of the intricate nature of the storylines. But you might just land in with an idea that the producer loves. On the other hand it might be a futile gesture and your letter will end in the bin.

"Most of the casting for the popular serials and series happens when the actor or actress is noticed in some other role. There is no short cut really. You have to get yourself on stage or screen somewhere, somehow, then in a subtle way, wave and say...look, aren't I clever? Aren't I brilliant? Employ me."

Miss X says there are no short cuts, meaning that to get into acting you have to clock up some sort of training and experience. But people have come into the soapie game from all sorts of angles...some of them highly unusual. Like Leslie Grantham, once the 'Dirty Den' of EastEnders who became interested in acting while serving a jail sentence for the murder of a taxi driver in Germany. Another star of that same soap, Mike Reid, was a stand-up comic before taking the part of Frank Butcher. For a man with no formal acting background, didn't he do well?

Jason Donovan came into the game in the face of fierce opposition from his actor father Terence. He recalls "Dad kept saying to me 'don't do it. Don't become an actor'. He was worried for me because the business is so unstable. At this stage in my life he'd been at it for 25 years and there were times when he was out of work for months. But there's something so irresistible about acting when you've been around it. I just had to have a go."

So at 18 young Jason pitched into Neighbo*urs* as Scott Robinson, and the rest, as we say, is history. His father would still prefer for him to be a lawyer or a draftsman or anything when the prospects are more steady. This is a typical reaction of a showbiz parent...protection of the young. But I can see why Jason got the job in Ne*ighbours*. And Kylie Minogue. I first met them in the late 80's when I was producing The Logies, Australia's TV Oscars ceremony. They walked towards me down a corridor, hand in hand. The Australian soaps dish up some beautiful young people and this was your classic couple. She was tiny and cute and pretty and you just wanted to scoop her up in your arms and hug her...in the nicest possible way of course. He was a bit bigger—not much—blonde, wholesome and polite and you just knew he'd be so kind about your wife's apple pie if you invited him home.

I started this chapter being a bit unkind about actors, and here I am saying nice things about Kylie and Jason. I must admit I've met a few other actors who were great people and didn't preen in mirrors and talk about wonderful they were. James Cagney was one. So was David Niven. I got to deal with both stars while working on the Parkinson chat show series. Cagney couldn't have been less like his tough guy image. A true gentleman. And Niven was a delight. He delivered terrific and irreverent stories about Hollywood and his life in general. Far from being vain, he poked fun at himself mercilessly. The only time he looked in the mirror was to see if his toupee was on straight.

If you are going to hit it big one day in acting, please be like James Cagney or David Niven. Or Kylie and Jason for that matter.

GET OUT AND ABOUT

I've described television as a heavily defended castle, and the fortresses with the toughest fortifications are in the big capital cities like London, Manchester and Birmingham. This is where most of the well-known and highly popular programmes are made. By the time you have made the definite decision that you are going to be on TV, this is where you'll want to be. But as a raw newcomer with little or no experience of telly, you'll wear your knuckles bare rapping on the underside of the closed drawbridge.

More often than not you are going to have to get out of town, or go abroad. There you will find that the castles are smaller, the occupants less defensive. On a good day they might even leave the drawbridge down for you. And they are still in the business of making television programmes. There are cameras and scripts and make-up and opportunities to put ideas, and yourself, on screen.

Once you have a bit of practical know-how in the trade, it is much easier to storm the ramparts of the bigger castles. This is what I did back in the sixties. Having had no luck with the big British TV companies I took the advice of a producer working in what was then Rhodesia. He said "get out to the New World. You are more likely to be given a break".

How right he was. I didn't fancy his neck of the woods, southern Africa, so I headed for Australia instead. Within weeks of hitting Sydney I struck gold. A new TV station, Channel Ten, had just opened and they were looking for staff. I walked into the foyer, asked to see the news editor, and was hired on the spot.

That's what I love about Australia. They'll give you a go. Here was a young pom, with only weekly local newspaper experience, and I am let into the magical and thrilling and often dangerous world of television news. It was one of the happiest and most exciting periods of my life. They put me on firstly as a scriptwriter, then after a matter of days set me loose as an on-camera reporter. There I was, out on the big stories, sticking microphones under people's noses, chasing cops as they chased bank robbers, filming dramatic reports from the scene of bushfires as flames licked around my shirt tails.

Then, as now, compared to stuffy, classbound Britain, things are a lot less restricted in Australian television and radio. At Channel Ten in those days there were no union lines drawn across jobs. On some weekends, when cutting room staff failed to make it in to work from the beach or barbie, I'd get to edit my own film. In the land of the dreaded Pom that would have brought the whole station to a standstill with a paralysing strike over demarcation. On other days I got to shoot film as second cameraman on a big story. Again, absolutely unheard of back in Old Blighty.

Over the years, during various stints in Australia, I have always picked up valuable new experience or contacts. I learned documentary-making there. I also broke into the chat show scene, where journalism and showbusiness meet up. It's called 'info-entertainment' these days and is still my main breadwinner. Because I happened to be in Australia at the right time and had knowledge of writing, and how to structure and produce interviews on behalf of a star host, I got to work with great talents like Dave Allen, John Cleese, David Frost and Michael Parkinson. The Parky connection was particularly beneficial in enabling me to finally breech the walls of the big BBC castle in London. In fact, the television centre at White City is a circular concrete doughnut which is not unlike a fort, in appearance and mentality.

It happened like this. I helped produce and research Mike's first Australian chat show series. They were a big success. When Mike heard I was returning to Britain he asked whether I would like to work on his BBC series. I said "too bloody right, cobber". Back at White City, he had a word in the right ear, the drawbridge clanged down, and there was me where I'd always wanted to be...at the Beeb.

Mobility and flexibility are important. Be prepared to travel around the world for opportunities, but don't expect to walk right into the plum job just because you've packed a suitcase. In most countries there are various levels of broadcasting, ranging from big deal prime time to country-rural. In Sydney I was lucky enough to score with a major metropolitan channel, but I was equally prepared to go out into the bush and work on a smaller country station.

Heading off to newer countries would also include the U.S.A. of course, and at the top level, television there would probably be the hardest to crack anywhere in the world. We're talking serious competition here. Even so, the territory is huge, and

Northern America—The States and Canada—have a multitude of smaller local stations which could well give you a break.

If you don't fancy foreign climes, then apply the same let's-start-small attitude to the home scene. Regional television provides an excellent training ground in television work, off camera and on. A whole host of famous performers like Terry Wogan and Sue Lawley learned their craft out in the sticks. Jenny Hull, who co-hosts How Do They Do That? came up from the BBC regional station TV South-East and beat a lot of strong competition at the audition to win her spot partnering Desmond Lynam. If you are any good, and have ambition, then you will use these outposts as a spring board. Television is a small world. Outposts can be signposts. If you're twinkling up there in Tyneside, word'll get around. Some big shot in The Smoke will ask to see a tape to find out what the fuss is all about.

These days there are so many other opportunities outside the main bigtime broadcasters. There's satellite TV for instance, like Sky. The audiences are small compared with the land-based channels, the hours long, the pay relatively low. But it is still telly, and if you finish up on camera you will get noticed by the big wigs if you are any good. Cable TV is catching on too, This is even more small-time that satellite, but again there are cameras and programme-makers and a ready market for ideas. The experience you will gain could be invaluable.

It doesn't matter how small the outfit is just so long as you get to know the tools of the trade, and how to use them. Hospitals, colleges of further education and big companies often have their own closed-circuit TV channels these days. Get in there and play. And learn. Television performing is like anything else that is difficult. You need somewhere to practise. And preferably experts to teach you There is a fine art in peering down the barrel of a camera and making yourself look convincing when you come out the other end on someone's TV screen. The first time anyone tries it they almost always have an unnatural, glazed look in their eyes. It is a most unwelcoming sight for the viewer.

When training people in on-camera technique you have to encourage them to imagine that the camera is another human being, preferably someone they know and are comfortable with. A few years ago one of my mates, a famous American producer, was hired to teach an Australian prime minister television techniques. He tended to come across on the nation's screens as a startled rodent. The politician was told by his tutor to imagine the camera was someone he loved deeply. He was asked who this was. The assumption was that the PM would nominate his high-profile and rather sexy wife. Instead he named...his pet cat. It worked.

So, you need to master the camera in the proper studio setting, with the correct degree of lighting, sound, and under the sort of tension that normally goes with real television. It is not something you can achieve in your loungeroom with your camcorder balanced on a stool and with you reading from papers strewn over your coffee table.

You'll also want to clock up a fair bit of mileage on the invaluable cheating device which gives the impression that presenters are talking so cleverly off the tops of their heads, where in fact they are reading a script. There are various systems with names like Autocue and Teleprompt, which all have the same effect. Words typed in by the operator are projected on a screen suspended directly in front of the camera, and can be read while the performer looks directly down the lens.

This is where telly is a lot harder than you would imagine. The way you look into the camera is critical. It is called your eyeline. If your gaze is off kilter the viewer will feel you are talking to someone else. The secret of success in this business is to convince everyone in the room that you are addressing them and no-one else. The old-fashioned prompting machines were tricky. They were basically big paper toilet rolls which unravelled to one side of the lens. You had to be very clever not to let your eyes swivel to that particular side . This was fatal back home in the living room, where the viewer would think you were addressing the next person along on the sofa.

Even with the modern prompter, you can move your eyes in a way to suggest that you are reading a script. And the spell is broken. It is also crucial that you are on good terms with the operator, who, if properly skilled, will run the words through on your screen at just the right speed. A bit too quick or a shade slow and you are dead meat.

You find all this out the hard way, under battle conditions. And if you plan a career as a bigtime TV star you are going to have to have all these things under control. So unless you are very, very lucky, or have extra-special contacts, or are sleeping with a powerful executive (more about that later), you are not going to get the experience you need at the studios of the BBC in London or NBC in Los Angeles. It's all going to happen out there at parish level.

Which is why I keep coming back to the idea of travelling abroad to learn the ropes. There are TV stations in every corner of the globe which might give you a break...from Austria to Zimbabwe. In my case it happened to be The Antipodes, which is about as far away from home as any Englishman can get. It was a lucky choice, because for a country with such a small population Australia has made a big impact on the international TV scene. Look at the success of Neighbours and Home and Away, and performers like Barry Humphries, Clive James and Rolf Harris.

The joy, to me, of Australian television is that on the major national networks you are working to top international standards with all the latest equipment and highly-professional crews, yet there is the sort of informality and unrestricted opportunities that in other countries you would normally get in local TV. Which means of course that if you actually go Bush to the small stations you have even more fun.

Television is just one example of a general sense of freedom and risk-taking which prevails in Australia. They'll give you a go. Take the case of Jimeoin. He comes from Northern Ireland and is fast making a name for himself on the international comedy scene. When Jimeoin arrived in Oz his last job had been as a surveyor in London. One night he was at a pub in Sydney where comics get up and do their stuff. Newcomers are encouraged. Urged on by his companions, who had sussed how naturally funny the Irish boy was, Jimeoin got up on stage and did a brilliant routine. He'd never faced an audience before.

Within weeks he was doing regular comedy gigs,

and within months was appearing on television. Now, although still in his twenties, Jimeoin has his own television series on national television in Australia. The point of this story is that as Jimeoin was so far away from his normal habitat that he dared something he certainly would not have tried in Ireland or London.

What happened to Jimeoin was sheer luck. In most cases you are going to have to push to get that break. And travel. Not just to Australia but around your own country or your continent or the whole world. It's a bit like prospecting for gold. You don't keep panning away on the same stretch of river if you haven't struck a nugget. Sooner or later you'll arrive somewhere where your face fits...on a television screen.

NOW FOR THE GOOD NEWS

If you have the right temperament and talent, you could end up in television news. And in terms of on-camera work, this can mean very exciting and lucrative times. Of all the jobs which offer the candidate the chance to see the world and meet interesting people, news has to grab the biscuit. As a telly reporter, one day you are covering an earthquake in Peru, the next you are thrusting a microphone up President Clinton's nose as he makes a state visit to China.

Television can make big stars out of newsfolk. They become household names. And heroes. Reporters like Martin Bell, Kate Adie and Mike Nicholson are genuinely brave people. They stand there in the world's battlefields, speaking their pieces while bullets whistle past their ears and shells thud into the ground beside them. Then, as they get a bit older and tired of the road, veteran reporters can make a bid for the newscaster's desk, and present the bulletins like Trevor McDonald, Martyn Lewis and Peter Sissons.

Mind you, for old operators who are used to an exciting life on the road, the lack of activity can be disastrous. Boredom led the late newscaster Reginald Bosanquet to booze. I saw it for myself when I worked at ITN as a scriptwriter. Reggie, who had once been a fine reporter, had so little to do in the afternoons he'd duck out and find somewhere to have a quiet drink. He'd turn up in time for the bulletin, nicely charged. In fact, later in his career he'd actually be sozzled on air. This was around the time when colour TV was catching on in a big way. Many puzzled viewers spent ages fiddling with their controls, and actually called the repair man, because when they saw Reggie they couldn't believe anyone would have a face that hue. But let this not deter you. Most newscasters these days are pillars of sobriety. The news business is too competitive for them to be otherwise.

Right at the beginning of the book I was encouraging you to look at all the types of on-camera roles available in the television industry to see which job would suit you, and we touched on news and currents affairs. By now you should have a clearer idea what it is you are cut out for. You'll certainly have some sort of inner stirrings at the mention of news work. I knew when I was a kid that one day I would be a reporter, and I reckon it is vocational.

If you think you might be that way inclined, let me hark back to a few simple questions I posed earlier and add a few extra. Are you genuinely interested in what is going on around you, not only in your own country but abroad? When a fire engine screams past in the other direction, are you tempted to make a rapid U-turn and follow it? Can you sense that there are stories happening in your neighbourhood or in your line of work which could or should be printed in a newspaper or broadcast on the airwaves? Do you pick the fact that more often than not politicians are talking a load of bullshit ? Do you shout angry questions at them when they are on radio or TV? If you are answering 'yes' to these questions then you probably belong in a newsroom. So how do you go about getting there?

Right up the very front of this little saga I said how I'd written to the BBC for a job when I was a young and keen lad and they hadn't even replied to my letters. This was in the Sixties and I had completed a three-year apprenticeship as a cub reporter on a North London local newspaper. I was ready to take on the world, but the Beeb didn't want to know about me. In those days you'd only get a look-in if you had Eton, Roedean and Oxbridge behind you, and preferably a Godparent who was a governor of the Corporation.

While mapping out this chapter I thought I'd check with the BBC news department to see how things stood in the Nineties. I've got to admit that I was pleasantly surprised at what I heard. There are still miles and miles of those bloody forms to fill in. But they were prepared to consider anyone with news experience or aptitude and education wasn't necessarily an issue. A degree certainly wasn't a condition of hiring. Neither did you have to be sponsored by an archbishop or field marshall.

Aptitude is the key word here. It means you are cut out for the job, you have a nose for news. O.K., so you think you are right for the job, how do you go about getting the experience? The answer is, look around you and notice where news is needed, and you will be surprised how many outlets there are. Here's just a few to give you a kickstart...company house journals, sports club newsletters, residents association pamphlets, local newspapers and a whole range of magazines covering specialised subjects from computers and model aircraft to carpentry and travel.

It's a case of start real small if you've never done reporting before, then build rapidly as you get the hang of it. With the house journal at work, for instance, find something which the whole company might be interested in knowing, trot along to whoever edits the paper, and suggest that you write an article. You will probably be given a warm welcome. You'll find, as you progress, that editors are always on the look-out for good stories, whether it be for a staff magazine or a national newspaper and television bulletin.

So, what constitutes an office story? Well, you might have a novel scheme in the buying department to keep life fresh. You swap desks around every month. Nice little angle here about a suspicious garment left in a colleague's draw. Didn't know old Pete was into fishnet stockings. It might be that Pam is so frustrated with the new computer that she's using her dad's ancient mechanical portable to type simpler documents. So much for progress.

When you've got the story you've got to present it in the right way. Here the editor will help, particularly if you have never written or reported before. You could well be asked to rejiggle your first attempt, possibly adding in some extra information. Don't get on your high horse. Listen, act...learn. Although this whole exercise is about making you a telly star, be reassured that most television and radio reporters start in print. There are so many more outlets, and lots more opportunities to get a good, solid grounding in news gathering and presenting.

On my first week of local newspaper reporting I covered the drama of a freak whirlwind which deroofed several houses in peaceful Bush Hill Park—that made the front page lead—a flower show, a couple of weddings and the search for a milk bottle thief. Boy, didn't I think I was special. All of 19, I had the trilby hat, the trench coat and the Senior Service cigarette perched in Humphrey Bogart style at the corner of my mouth. Mind you, the hat and fag would often blow away as I pedalled my patch on an old Raleigh pushbike. And there would be times when I would forget to remove the cycle clips at the scene of the story, which would spoil the Bogart image a bit.

The point is that whether you are wielding pencil and notebook or camera and microphone, the reporting techniques are basically the same. You have to spot the story, get in there and cover it, often under very tricky circumstances. People might not want you around. They might try and throw you off the scent, or kick you off the premises. You have to get the knack of interviewing subjects in a particular way so you get the story you are after.

As I said in the beginning, I got my break on the local paper by sending in my own reports. No harm in apply this terror tactic to telly. Get yourself a camcorder and try a few stories on your local news service. Don't hit the BBC or ITN straight off. Walk before you can run. And don't worry if they are amateurish. Earlier we were dealing with the casting directors in TV drama, and how home videos weren't helpful. In news it is quite different. They will be looking for signs of initiative and a news sense. If you happen to have your camcorder with you when something really big happens, like an armed robbery or a plane crash, you could have your tape sold at a high price, and get a job thrown in.

I'm on my favourite hobby horse again, but this is so important when going after your first break. Make sure that whatever you produce is original and interesting. Don't copy. Don't ape a story that has already been covered. Look around your neighbourhood. Find something no-one else has done. It might be the tramp or bag lady who was once a war hero. Or a nutter who reckons he has a Martian in his shed. If a story doesn't come to a reporter then the reporter goes out and finds it.

Also, remember what we were saying earlier about infiltration. See if your local TV newsroom needs some unpaid help. Offer yourself for work experience. If you succeed but only get to make the coffee and stack files and tapes, ask in a firm but nice way if you could please go out with a news crew when they cover a story. Unless the bosses are complete bastards, you'll get the nod. And if you do, watch everything that takes place. See how the reporter prepares. Note how the story is shot. Try and get pally with the journalist and ask if you can buy him or her a drink one day when off duty. Don't hide your curiosity. They'll know what you are after. If they are good reporters curiosity will be their main tool.

As far as your own personality is concerned, there is absolutely no point in you considering television reporting as a career unless you are cut out for it. The job is very tough, very competitive—some other bugger from a rival station is always trying to get there first—and your personal and family life will be perpetually chaotic. You are rarely at home, for ever on the move. Don't think you can sit down with the holiday brochures in December and plan your summer holiday fortnight in Marbella for the following August. You might well be in Delhi at that time covering a riot. Or at the South Pole with some expedition.

I don't want to labour the jeopardy angle, but reporting can be bloody dangerous. Journalists get wounded and killed in action. You might discover you have phobias you never knew you suffered from. Like fear of fire for instance. Within a few months of starting on my local paper I had to cover a huge factory blaze. A reporter arrived from a national newspaper. He sat trembling in his car, muttering "I can't stand fires." I finished up giving him all the information he needed. He never left his vehicle.

It was while covering another factory inferno in Sydney with a television news crew that I first discovered free flight. One minute we were going through this fence, next thing I was hurled backwards about thirty feet, over a stream, landing on my back with no wind left in my lungs. The power was extraordinary. It was as if a giant hand had tossed me in the air. As I lay on my back battling for breath my cameraman flew past above my head, his clothes and hair on fire and his camera still jammed to his eye. We had ignored a fireman's warning, as news crews always do, and had copped the full blast of a warehouse full of chemicals exploding. A dozen steps closer and we would have both been dead.

If none of this puts you off, then go for it. Because I have got to tell you that there is no more exciting and satisfying a way to earn a quid than reporting. You get the thrills, the fun, the status, a reasonable pay packet. And occasionally you get to change the course of history. Can you ask for more than that?

THE GLAMOUR ROAD... AND OTHER ROUTES

If you have the looks and the right amount of push, you can fast-track it to screen fame. To demonstrate how this can be done, I am taking two real-life success stories. Both subjects are girls, which doesn't come as a great surprise to me, because in my opinion women have the best faces, are much sexier than men...and are a hundred times more persistent when it comes to chasing fame.

The first case history concerns Jane March, the so-called 'Sinner from Pinner' after her scorching sex scenes in a movie, The Lover. This is a kid who left school at 18 with no GCSE's and at only 5ft 2ins had all the physical allure of a stick insect. Yet at 21 she has swopped her semi-detached in one of London's most boring suburbs for a house in the Hollywood Hills, a groovy film director husband,

and a group of in-crowd friends who include Bruce Willis and Demi Moore.

How did she do it? Answer: the modelling route. There's nothing new about the method. Twiggy took that road back in the Sixties. Even earlier Roger Moore and Brigitte Bardot were advertising sweaters and Audrey Hepburn graced the fashion pages of up-market fashion magazines. What usually happens is that a director will pick up a publication, see an interesting face and/or body, and reach for the phone.

Which is exactly what happened to Jane March. As a teenager she was tiny and had matchstick legs and a chubby face. But despite her physical shortcomings she was desperately ambitious. She knew she wanted to be a model. At 13 she scandalised respectable Pinner by going out and getting a perm. Every night she pinned her ears back with elastic bands to stop them sticking out and she and her mates would pore over fashion magazines, their young faces caked with make-up.

One day Jane took the train up to London and started flogging around the modelling agencies. She was given some pretty blunt rejections. It was usually 'thanks sweetheart but you are too small'. Now we're getting to the nub. This is the part of the story to pay close attention to. It is a common strand with most successful stars, and you must follow their example. Jane didn't give up. She wouldn't take no for an answer. You read the biographies of a hundred famous people—actors, actresses, pop stars, best selling authors—and around 95%, at some stage or other, will have been battering on a lot of closed doors. It happened, for instance, to The Beatles. You don't need any other examples.

Finally the famous Storm agency listened to the determined rappings of those tiny knuckles, and gave Jane a break. She started getting work almost straight away. French director Jean-Jacques Annaud spotted her on the cover of Just Seventeen Magazine, and described her as "a little girl who looked as bored as a rat by being photographed, with revolt in her eyes".

Then the whirlwind started. Annaud cast Jane March as the 15-year-old heroine in his film The Lover even though she had not one jot of acting experience. She was whisked off to steamy Vietnam for six months of even steamier on-camera sex. The movie hit the world cinema scene like an erotic mortar shell. Now in Hollywood they talk of Jane as the next Sharon Stone.

The fact that our Sinner from Pinner is now a big movie star and this is a book about being a TV star is not really a problem. It is all to do with grabbing fame. And anyway, Jean's movies will eventually finish up on telly...heavily censored no doubt.

By becoming a model, she took the first vital steps in getting herself noticed by the right people. Of course modelling is a glitzy world unto itself. You can be a big star without going anywhere near an acting role. Look at super-models like Naomi Campbell and Elle McPherson. In fact Elle La Belle is now moving towards grease paint and drama. But only after a good ten years whereby she has been on the front pages of newspapers and magazines and on just about every major TV chat show in the world just on the strength of a modelling career. In fact, so fascinating is the subject that a whole book on How To Be A Model is planned in this current series. It will contain all sorts of fascinating revelations for you would-be Kings and Queens of the catwalk.

Next we are going to look at another dynamic lady with the unlikely name of Mariella Frostrup. She came to TV stardom not via the modelling route, but making sure she was in the right pace at the right time, with the right people. And making use of her natural beauty. The scene is The Cannes Film Festival, and at one of the swisher hotels, a group of influential movie folk, including TV critic Barry Norman, are sipping drinks around a poolside bar. Suddenly they are joined by a stunning blonde wearing nothing but a very brief bikini and a puckered brow. "I seem to have locked myself out of my room" she simpered in her husky, come-to-bed voice. "What am I going to do?"

Says a chap who was in the group: "She could have gone to reception and got a spare key. We didn't fall for that nonsense. Naturally she joined us at the bar. That was what she'd planned all along. She was gorgeous and she knew it. And no ordinary Cannes bimbo either. We all knew that here was a girl who was going places".

And going places Ms Frostrup did. At the time this goes to the printers she presents The Little Picture Show on ITV and there is talk of her having her own late-night chat show on the same channel. She also appears as a panellist on the trendy Have I Got News For You and has her own column in a national newspaper. Not bad for a girl who has had no real grounding in either journalism or broadcasting.

She comes from a pretty exotic background. The daughter of a Scottish artist mother and a Norwegian journalist father, Mariella grew up in Ireland. She realised at 14 she wanted to be a star. At 16 she came across to London, lived in a squat, worked as a barmaid and started banging on influential doors. Does this have a familiar ring by now? It should.

Eventually she got the break, helping out in a mobile recording studio owned by the Rolling Stones. Now she was rubbing shoulders with pop stars. She set her sights on Richard Jobson, lead singer with The Skids, romanced him and finally married him. She was 18, he was 20. "Mariella didn't wait around for Richard to propose because she knew he wasn't going to" a friend recalls, "So she proposed to him".

As it happened, the marriage was to be short-lived. Mariella's fame quickly outstripped her husband's. She moved into the record business as a press officer and became very active on the party scene. She handled the PR for groups like Tears For Fears and Dire Straits. Her boss of that time, publicist Chris Poole, says of her success: "It was her looks and her personality. To be frank the men fancied her and she certainly knew how to use her personality. She had no formal training and when she wrote press releases I had to correct her spelling and grammar".

Mariella began to fancy herself as a TV presenter, and of course she was perfectly placed. She was already in with the right people. Pop stars and TV producers were her constant party mates. She was famous by association with the famous. Stephen Garrett, who gave her a job presenting Channel Four's Big World Cafe, puts it as simply as this; "People involved with the programme knew her, although she was just plugging records at the time. Someone suggested: 'try Mariella' so I did."

You might not be able to stand a bar of either Jane March or Mariella Frostrup but you have got to give them both full marks for effort. They engineered their own opportunities for stardom, cashing in on assets like looks and personality. And of course sex appeal. They left nothing to chance. They realised, quite rightly, that the chances of being stopped in the street by a TV producer were virtually nil.

Samantha Fox can puff her chest out and say she blazed her own way to stardom. And what a chest, too. It was this magnificently-proportioned section of her body which earned her fame and fortune as a page three girl. She was smart enough to push this exposure beyond the flaunting of pert nipples to TV and film work and recording contracts.

I was involved in Samantha's first major television appearance back in the eighties when she came on the Wogan chat show. Talking beforehand with her and her mum I was impressed with the honest and uncomplicated attitude they had to the whole page three thing. Samantha, who was still a teenager at the time and barely out of school, said "I was a skinny, rather plain kid. Then one morning I woke up with these enormous knockers". The family reacted as if they had discovered an oil well in the back garden. This was a God-sent gift which had to be exploited. And why not?

They could have gone the other way. They could

have wrapped Samantha up in baggy, shapeless sweaters, and kept her indoors on hot days. Instead she bared her breasts to the nation. It was her decision in the end. No-one forced her. Because on that fateful morning Sam looked in the mirror and saw her burgeoning figure and realised she could be a star. And like Jane and Mariella she went for it.

They did it our way.

THE CASTING COUCH

This true story was told to me by a colleague and it happened to her when she had just started in television. She was a floor assistant on a major comedy series and her job was to shepherd the cast between their dressing rooms, the make-up and costume departments and the studio, bringing cups of tea and other refreshments when required.

One night, just before a recording, she was looking for a particular actress who was a regular in the series. Having tried the usual dressing rooms with no luck, she branched off into a hitherto unexplored corridor. Entering one of the rooms, she walked in on an amazing sight. The actress in question was there with the producer of the show, a gentleman of advanced years. He was lying on the sofa with his trousers around his ankles and she was sitting on a chair beside him, dress open at the top and breasts bared. Her hand was moving rhythmically in the region of his lap.

The poor girl stood frozen with embarrassment. The actress smiled sheepishly and, much to the intruder's amazement, kept pumping. The producer, ever the gentleman, said calmly: "you should have knocked, my dear, but never mind. We shan't be long". The floor assistant backed quietly out of the room, closed the door, then bolted down the corridor. She didn't mention the incident until weeks later when, drinking in the studio bar with a long-standing member of the production team, she let it slip. "He laughed" she recalled "He said: 'Oh, she always does that for him. That's how she keeps her job on the show' ".

You'll either be totalled horrified by this story, or you'll think, so what, that's what Cheryl does, only worse, with the regional sales director to make sure she gets allocated all the best territories. Or maybe it is your mate Steve, who regularly gives one to personnel manager Beryl in the sick room after lunch in order to keep his job as foreman of the stock yard even though he has the organisational ability of a punchdrunk turkey.

There is nothing new about trading sexual favours for job prospects and career advancement. In Showbiz it is particularly rife. We call it the casting couch syndrome. The expression harks back to the dark old days of Hollywood when producers, directors and agents would use the sofa or couch in their office to "audition" a budding actress. The deal was often spelt out to the girls "give me your body, Babe and I'll give you the part."

Similar propositions are still being put to would-be stars and it is not just man to woman and woman to man but man to man and woman to woman. And locations for the ensuing hanky panky are a lot more imaginative than a mere couch. We're talking now about sex in luxury hotel suites, executive jets, jacuzzis, the back seats of stretched limousines and on private Caribbean beaches.

Celebrities tend to be kinkier than normal folk. One famous international singing star, when casting chorus girls for his TV specials, would give preference to the candidates who would agree to strip off and straddle a large stone lion in his apartment, then let him have his way with them from the pillion seat. It all sounds pretty uncomfortable to me but it helped get a few ladies some time in the limelight.

So, how is this all going to affect you in your quest for TV stardom? Is it going to come to the crunch where fame and fortune will hinge on whether or not you will hop out of your knickers or Y-fronts? Well, the likelihood is that the subject will probably crop up at some stage or other when a person in power suggests, either directly or with a bloody great hint, that your chances of getting on camera would be greatly enhanced by agreeing to sex.

Whether you consent or not, remember that no single person in the television industry has the power to make you or break you. They can make life difficult for you, and block progress down one particular path. But then you duck sideways and take another route. I'm a great believer in the theory that true talent triumphs whatever the obstacles.

A great deal of bonking goes on in television which has nothing to do with casting couches or career improvement. Affairs in the workplace are commonplace, but in TV they seem to be of epidemic proportion. I think it must be something to do with the danger and excitement of programme-making, particularly when you are working live. I've often compared it to combat duties in a fighter squadron. When the time nears for transmission and everyone's nerves are stretched to breaking point, it's like strapping on the old chute and scrambling for the Spitfire.

In times of war and television production, teams bond together under pressure as a family. Staff turn to each other for physical as well as professional comfort. So the point I am making is that when you enter the business you are going to find a lot of sex about anyway. Which doesn't alter the fact that there is a big difference between having an affair with a colleague because you fancy them rotten, and bonking someone in higher places who is promising to help you get on screen.

My advice is as follows. You are going to make it as a TV star because of your abilities. No television executive in his or her right mind will let you anywhere near a camera if you are no good. Their jobs depend on making the right decision. This won't stop some unscrupulous bosses from making you false promises in order to take sexual advantage.

I'm a great believer in instinct in these cases. When faced with any sort of difficult decision, whether it is to go to bed with a producer or commit yourself to the purchase of a house, there will be a little voice inside you giving advice. You might have to strain the old inner ear, but it is there. Does this person seem genuine? Are they promising you too much too soon? Does the offer involve something highly unlikely, like your own music show to rival Michael Ball's, when your singing career adds up to warbling a hit pop song as you make the crew's coffee?

The trouble is, if your ego is considerably enlarged—and this tends to be the case with the type of people who become TV performers—you might well believe that you are ready for prime time telly now, even though you are only a lowly messenger and kettle boiler on a production team. And you are going to be in for a dreadful disappointment when, the morning after the night of passion, you are totally ignored in the office by the executive who only hours earlier was whispering hot and passionate things in your ear. On top of which you never hear another mention of your promised Saturday night starring role.

Should this happen, and you fall for the trick, handle it coolly. Don't look for retribution or revenge. Certainly don't blab it around the office. Those who actually believe you, won't care, and will think you are a prat for taking the bait. Then the boss will probably fire you for causing trouble in the office, or on a trumped-up charge that you are inefficient.

No, what you must do is to realise you have been duped, and learn from the experience. Just as if a conman has emptied your wallet or purse of money. You don't run after them with a gun or knife. You could finish up in trouble with the law and they'll almost certainly stay Scott free...in exactly the same way as the producer who ravaged you will maintain position and power and you will end up out in the street again.

Cope with it this way. Tell yourself you are a bloody fool for falling for such a trick. Vow you'll be wiser next time. And there could well be a next time, and a time after that, if word gets around that you are an easy lay, that you leap out of your clothes at the mere mention of facing a TV camera. All this works the other way, of course. I have seen youngsters enter the business who are like predators when it comes to seeking out people in power who might speed them along in their careers. If it means giving out with sex, then so be it. It's almost as if that is part of the job and you have to be good at it. Just like being best at a new office computing system so you'll be head of the queue for promotion.

Sex isn't nearly as special as it used to be. I pick up my newspaper and I read that girls from good homes and schools think nothing of working as call girls with escort agencies to help support themselves through university. With that sort of thinking, then you can understand why some ambitious candidates for an on-camera job wouldn't blink at offering sex if it might give them a break.

If you are tempted to take the carnal course in your career, just be warned that you might find yourself deeper in than you expected. We've already looked at the scenario where a producer has offered you your own prime time show in order to get a quick overnight bonk, then has dropped you abruptly like the proverbial hot cake. Terrible as this might sound, there is another twist to the plot which I find worse. He, or she, might give you some sort of break, then continue to expect sexual favours on a regular basis. You will have your first taste of fame...it might well be something unspectacular like wearing a spangled costume and pointing inanely at prizes on a game show. We call these "fridge strokers" in the telly business. In the meantime you know you are going to have to continue to service someone who you could well find very unattractive.

Then of course people are going to talk. Your reputation will spread. You might be offered another on-camera role a little more exciting than stroking fridges—stand in weather girl on the occasional early morning weekend shift, or the boy who wheels the barrel on set for a lucky dip. And, quite quickly, you might find the hard word being put on you in the dressing room and you realise you are expected to "pleasure" your new producer. You are, effectively, whoring. You are being passed around like a bit of meat. And if you don't come across they'll wonder why you do it for someone else and not for them. They could turn very nasty...and destructive.

If you are the type of person who definitely isn't inclined to give sex in return for career advancement, hold firm to your beliefs and don't buckle under pressure...or indeed threats. There might be times when you are propositioned by someone who, when rejected might snarl; "I'll ruin you...you'll never get anywhere in this business." Just remember what I said earlier. No one person has this sort of power. Don't give in to moral blackmail. Neatly sidestep your aggressor and move on somewhere else.

At the risk of sounding an old-fashioned puritan I'd sum up my feelings on this casting couch issue as follows. People who give their sexual favours for reasons other than love are prostituting themselves. Prostitutes will sell pleasure to a punter for money, but there's often someone in their life who they really love and with whom they really enjoy sex and no fee is involved. It has to be that way in television. To survive and indeed thrive our business you have really got to love it.

The other night another veteran producer and I were sitting exhausted at our desks after several consecutive 14-hour days. We agreed that we put up with the unsocial hours and all the other associated aggro because we loved television. If you've made some sort of progress by giving sex to powerful producers and other executives, sooner or later you could well lose respect for yourself, and the industry. You'll see television as a greedy fat punter and you'll go somewhere else to seek true love. If you have genuine talent, that would be a real pity.

HAVE I LEFT IT TOO LATE? OR AM I TOO EARLY?

Age is an important issue when considering a change of career. I don't reckon it should be, but that's the way most people think. You can't blame them, because so many jobs seem to impose age restrictions. In those newspaper ads for thrusting young sales personnel, the optimum age always seems to be set between 25 to 35. In most categories of employment the advertiser doesn't seem to be interested in anyone over 45.

What about television? Is it ever too late to have a shot at being a star? Well, as you've probably gathered if you have stayed with me this long, I have taken a positive line throughout, and I would say quite definitely that you are *never* too old to shine on telly. In fact, if some boringly predictable old company has slung you on the scrap heap because they reckon you are past it at 50, then maybe you could give Nicholas Parsons a run for his money. It's about time someone did.

The fact that Old Nick is in his late sixties and still earning a good quid on the screen is some indication of how flexible the telly game is when it comes to age. At the other extreme you get toddlers pulling in nice fat cheques for their mums by modelling disposable nappies in commercials. If you have what it takes, and the idea and the timing is right, you can burst forth into telly stardom at any point in your life.

There is one point of entry which is all but blocked off if you are 30-plus and that is the tactic of joining a production team as a general dogsbody or messenger. Junior jobs in television do tend to go to younger people. And any rate, you get to an age where dignity is important and you would feel uncomfortable and humiliated brewing endless cups of tea and coffee and running around town delivering and collecting packages.

Specialist knowledge in one particular area is a great route in for the more mature would-be star. Remember Barbara Woodhouse and her catchphrase "walkies"? She had a highly distinctive way of dealing with dogs and it made her a megastar in her sixties. In Keith Floyd's case it is food and he didn't hit the limelight in a big way until he had turned 40. I still mourn the passing of the irrepressible Ffye Robertson. Travel was this great Scot's stock in trade, and he was at it well into his eighties. At the time he died Ffye was desperately trying to persuade the BBC to let him take a train trip across China with a camera crew.

We've actually covered the subject of specialisation earlier in the book, if all this seems to be ringing a bell. I took the example of someone who reckoned he or she was God's gift to home improvement, and was battering on the door of a breakfast show producer for a break. Age didn't come into it at this stage, and there is no reason to assume that the budding do-it-yourself guru wasn't 70-plus. If you are good enough and original enough, no clever producer will hold age against you.

And that is the crunch. You have to dare to be different. People have done doggie stuff on telly before, but not like Barbara Woodhouse, in her upper-class bossy way. Floyd makes food fun, and pokes jibes all the time at his cameraman. The secret is to think of a particular subject to deal in, but treat it in a particular way. Adopt a style that no-one else has thought of. When you are specialising, age can be a huge advantage. It can mean experience, years of knowledge.

What to specialise in? Well, what are you good

at? It's a bit like going through the yellow pages. You will score if you deal with a subject that touches most of our lives, and then throw some light on it. The list is pretty close to endless...clothes, food, cars, money, astrology, sex, sport, science, gardening, child-rearing, alternative medicine, airplanes, ghosts, office politics, marriage guidance, films, travel, sailing, climbing...etcetera etcetera. The absolutely golden rule, bearing in mind most of these subjects are already covered, is to tackle them in your own special way. No copying. And make sure you know your chosen subject really well.

Then of course there is acting. Earlier, in the chapter on becoming a soap opera star, we were hearing from the casting director, Miss X, about how to get yourself noticed by her and her colleagues in drama. During my session with Miss X she told me that there were possibilities for actors and actresses of all ages. In fact, sometimes the older roles were the hardest to cast, simply because there wasn't the range of players to choose from. So, if you are fiftyish and feeling a bit bashful about enrolling in your local drama group, don't hold back. One of the nicest and most interesting stars I have ever dealt with in showbusiness was the late Irene Handl, the character actress who featured hilariously in so many Peter Sellers movies. Irene picked up her first professional acting job when she was well into her forties.

We've talked about comedy, too, and how making people laugh can get you on the box. It's a fact that comedians get better with age, even though some of them don't realise it. I remember once keeping Mel Brooks company in the make-up room just before he went on a Wogan show. Suddenly he turned and grabbed my arm, and his face was frozen with fear. He croaked:"I'm fifty-six years of age and I've got to go out there and be funny. I don't think I am funny." He then went to do battle with the old Irishman and was absolutely hilarious.

Two points from this little story to reassure and encourage late starters in the comedy game. Firstly, fear never leaves you. In fact it is a vital element in a performer's life...a sort of creative cattle prod. So, if you are 45 and you are thinking of facing your first audience with a funny speech or routine and your knees are playing drum solos down there, don't think that you are any different from Mel Brooks. Get out there and do it. You'll feel absolutely wonderful once you have got your first laugh. There's no drug to touch it. And remember what we've been saying earlier...comedy is a great way to crack the TV scene.

The other point is that Mel gets funnier with the passing of the years because of the experience he has been building up, and the various things that have been happening to him. The best comics are the ones who absorb all the bodyblows than life can aim, just like we try and do, and they reassure us that we are not alone in our frustration. Dave Allen does this brilliantly. He, like Mel Brooks, improves with age. So do Bob Monkhouse and Jimmy Tarbuck. Both have had hiccups in their careers in recent years, but have come back funnier than ever and strengthened by the experience. So, if you've built up a bit of bile working 20-odd years in a garage or in the thick of office politics at a bank, then you'll find you probably have a wealth of material to draw from when you come to write your first comedy routine.

Better a person enter the business as a mature and worldwise adult than a babe. I have a real problem with child stars and the damage fame can inflict on kids. The showbiz pressures, and the undue amount of attention focussed on the youngsters, can often have a devastating effect as they hit adulthood. I am still haunted by the memory of my first encounter with Lena Zavaroni. This was back in the Seventies, and Lena had won a big TV talent quest. She was a tiny, plump eleven-year-old of Scottish-Italian parents with a big booming voice and a totally enchanting manner.

At the time I met Lena she was about to be

launched in America, and I was helping to arrange her publicity campaign over there. The child had temporarily left her home in Scotland and was staying at her manager's luxury apartment in Mayfair. She showed me a wardrobe full of expensive dresses and said "Aren't these pretty...but I've been told I've got to lose a bit of weight before I can get into them". Lena moved on to her teens and developed a horrendous anorexia problem which was widely covered in the press and caused the poor kid much misery. I am not in a position to point the finger of blame at anybody, nor would I wish to. It would achieve nothing now, only maybe to warn parents to be very careful when letting their babes near showbiz.

You can't convince me that child stars lead normal lives. Hayley Mills once told me that she grew up barely able to read and write because her schooling was so badly neglected during those "golden" years when she was making hit movies like Tiger Bay, The Parent Trap and Pollyanna. And what about Drew Barrymore, the little cutie from E.T. She talks about her drink and drugs problem and staggering home from nightclubs in the early hours...when she was thirteen. What was her Mum doing? Wasn't anyone in control?

Child performers who become very famous usually mutate into monsters. I once talked to a veteran Hollywood performer who had worked on a couple of Shirley Temple movies in the thirties. What was Miss Dimples like, I asked? "Well," he drawled guiltily, "I used to fantasize a lot about what it would be like to strangle her. It was the only thing that kept me sane." I know how he must have felt. I once wanted to throttle Macaulay Culkin, or worse, but there was a whole stretch of the Pacific Ocean between us. I was in Melbourne and he was in Los Angeles and we were hooking up on a satellite interview for a TV show. A technical fault developed and a delay set in. Soon the little wart turned nasty. It wasn't a childish tantrum but the full Hollywood megastar "what's wrong with you bums down there, can't you get your effing act together" routine. I just longed to be across the waters, in that studio, and aiming a couple of good hard slaps against those insolent jug ears.

Master Macaulay is fast reaching the age where he will no longer be considered cute. His voice will break, he will sprout pimples, he will be forgotten by Hollywood producers. Thanks to a shrewd—and equally obnoxious—father, the lad should be alright for pocket money for the rest of his life. That's assuming Pa lets him near the pot of gold. Most likely, after enjoying so much attention for so long, he will feel neglected and disorientated. This is the hardest time for a former child star. Despite his awfulness during that satellite session, I wish Macaulay Culkin no ill will. I just hope he makes it to adulthood as a sane human being.

My honest advice to parents with star-struck kiddies who are desperate to get on telly is to do it all in a smallscale but sensible way. Let them have a shot at TV commercials. Normally the shooting schedule can be arranged around the child's schooling. How do you go about this? Again, use a bit of initiative. Phone around the child modelling agencies. They'll probably suggest you write in with a picture of your beloved brat. If they like what they see you'll be asked to bring your youngster to the office for a chat and a look-see. A lot of the bigger agencies also place kiddies in TV dramas too, so you'll be killing two birds with one stone.

The golden rule is to make it all seem like fun for the child if they do get work on screen, but never let them think they are superstars, and than school and normal life suddenly take second place. And any money they earn should go into a savings account for later in their lives, or used to help out the household budget if things are tight financially within the family. No sudden and ostentatious displays of wealth, like a gold-plated trail bike or Gucci dollies' pram. It won't go down too well in your neighbourhood, particularly if you live on a council estate.

Keep the tiny one on a tight rein. You don't want another Macaulay Culkin on your hands. Otherwise you'll ask the little darling to tidy the bedroom or get cracking on the homework and you'll be told "I need to talk to my agent first". Be warned. It is a nightmare which could come true.

FAME...A FICKLE BUTTERFLY

Now you are a telly star in waiting. Soon, if you have taken aboard all the good advice you've been getting recently, you'll be inside that celebrity castle. I have a few warnings. Don't worry, we're not ending on a downer. I just want you to know what life is going to be like for you in the limelight. I'm sure it won't put you off. In fact I hope you'll be better prepared.

Let's look at what fame really means. Well, for a start, you'll never be a normal person again. There is the recognition factor. Once you start appearing regularly on TV people will recognise you while you are out and about. The first time it happens you will probably get a huge buzz. You'll be fingering the white cabbages at your local Sainsburys and someone will smile and say "aren't you whatsisname?" The next few times will almost certainly be fun too. You'll get the feeling you are a celebrity. You'll sign an autograph or two. When you go to restaurants you will suddenly find you get better tables. You might well get your first write up in the press, with a flattering photo. Hey, this is something. Hollywood here I come.

Then the day will come when you just want to be left alone. You have a hangover and you look like you've just stepped off a slab at the local mortuary. Or you are having a screaming fight with your spouse or partner at the post office. Worse, you are out canoodling with someone who quite clearly isn't your spouse or partner. They, the public, will know because they've read all about you in the newspapers and magazines. They not only are aware of who you are supposing to be sleeping with, they also have knowledge of the type of toothpaste you use, the car you drive and what sort of underwear you prefer. Not to mention your starsign, your favourite alcoholic beverage and where your mother went to school.

When you become famous you become public property. Because you are beamed into people's homes through their television sets they feel they know you. "It is quite extraordinary," the Good Life actor Richard Briers once told me. "Strangers come up to me in the street and talk as if I am an old acquaintance. They also feel entitled to be quite critical. They'll say things like 'I thought you were a lot of rubbish on telly last night' without it occurring to them that this might be rude or offensive to me."

It can get physical, too. I was walking down Regent Street with Terry Wogan one day when a burly chap walked up to us, grabbed hold of Terry's midriff and gave it a good tug. "Bit of slack here, eh Tel? So much for the fight on flab". The famous Irishman side-stepped the man, and with a quick smile, kept walking. He behaved like he was used to it, and such minor assaults were part of the job.

When your personal life goes adrift, it is bad enough when you are an ordinary soul. If you are a telly star it can be a nightmare. These days, with so much competition in the popular press for juicy showbiz stories, you are given no sanctuary. A few years back Des O'Connor was going through some domestic trauma and we couldn't get scripts delivered to his flat because of the army of reporters and photographers banked up to his front door. More recently, when Michael Aspel was going through his much publicised marital upheaval, the This Is Your Life team thought they had found a haven for a quiet end-of-term lunch in a restaurant that had been closed to the general public. That didn't stop a press photographer suddenly springing from nowhere just as we were tucking into pudding. The

"Oh Christ" look of dejection on Michael's face was unforgettable.

With fame all sort of other things change too. You move into a new social circle. You might suddenly find your old friends too boring, or not glamorous enough. Or they in turn might find you have become insufferably big headed and flash. You could feel that your home and your car aren't smart enough for your newly-acquired stardom, and you undertake an expensive programme of change. Smarmy estate agents are suddenly showing you around expensive houses with gold-tapped jacuzzis and mini-golf courses in the back garden. You are getting trade-in prices for the trusty old Vauxhall Cavalier against a swish new BMW with a multi-speakered sound system that would do justice to the local cinema.

Being a popular television star you could get an inflated idea of your own importance. And the press doesn't help. Sharon decides to sling in her job at the Old Vic and from the size of the headlines you would think that World War Three had broken out. Well, EastEnders is watched by 15 million people. It's interesting to note that Sharon is very real to her fans, and the fact that she is played by an actress called Letitia Dean is all but overlooked.

Being in a popular soap or drama you can easily lose your sense of identity. Viewers really believe you are the character you play. Bet Lynch is Bet Lynch. Who the hell is this Julie Goodyear? Inspector Morse is very real to most people. They believe that even now he is slumped near his stereo, listening to classical music while the old Jag sits outside in the garage. John Thaw, the actor who played him, is another person. Who really wants to know about him. I find it all a bit spooky. Like I said earlier, who would want to be an actor?

And of course, fame can be a fickle butterfly. TV stardom is a precarious old trade by anyone's standards. Although the financial rewards can be brilliant when you are there at the top, job security is nil. In fact nil-minus. Suddenly you can fall out of favour. Your ratings start dropping for some reason or other. Maybe the public has tired of your act, or someone else has come along on another channel who is doing your kind of thing better. You fall out of favour with the producers' mafia, and suddenly your contract isn't renewed. How are you going to maintain the mortgage on the house with the gold-tapped Jacuzzi, and meet the monthly payments on the BMW?

But enough of all this doom and gloom. I've only painted this bleak picture to egg you on. If you are that determined to have a crack at the bigtime, this shouldn't put you off. It's a bit like the brave warrior setting off on a thrilling mission who has been warned to expect Ogres and snake-pits and steep mountains with crumbly paths. They are all obstacles that can be overcome with determination and bravery.

A final bit of advice. If you have set out to become a television star, believe in yourself. Keep in your mind a strong sense of who and what you want to be. Don't be swayed or deterred. If people smirk at your ambitions to get on camera, then use their cynicism as a spur to even harder effort, just to prove the point. You must convince yourself, and the industry, that there is no-one quite like you, and that the nation's television screens need you.

And do you know what? You're right.